Take-Home Learning Totes for Grades 1 and 2

by
Cheryl Sauls Taylor

illustrated by Gary Mohrmann
edited by Ellen Sussman

Cover by Gary Mohrmann

Copyright © 1993, Good Apple

ISBN No. 0-86653-768-6

Printing No. 98765432

Good Apple
1204 Buchanan St., Box 299
Carthage, IL 62321-0299

A Paramount Communications Company

Table of Contents

GA1471

How to Make "Take-Home Learning Totes"

In order to maximize the use of *Take-Home Learning Totes for Grades 1 and 2,* it is suggested that you make four to six copies of each kit so that several students may practice the same skill simultaneously. It is recommended that one of each kit be set aside to use for replacement pieces as they become worn or are lost.

Since making four to six of each kit is time-consuming, organize a mini workshop! Ask for parent volunteers or capable students in the upper grades to help after school. Reproduce the kit components so that each volunteer has a complete set. Make an extra set to have available in case of mistakes. As you make a kit, the parents or students make the same kit along with you. Within a short time, you will have four to six copies of each kit.

For each kit, you will need:
  one 9" x 12" (22.86 x 30.48 cm) (or larger) seal-top plastic bag
  one sandwich-size seal-top plastic bag or 6" x 9" (15.24 x 22.86 cm) manila envelope
    (to hold small pieces)
  one copy of tote activity sheet (identifies kit; lists contents and activities)
  one copy of each manipulative sheet
  copies of "Tote Notes" (homework slips–use is optional)

In addition, have on hand fine-line and broad-tipped, brightly colored and neon markers, scissors, stapler, cardboard or tagboard, laminating facilities, and file boxes for storing completed Learning Tote kits.

1. Using the tote activity sheet, select *one* colored marker to fill in the tote bag handle, "Return to" tag and the outline letters that name the kit. All kits of the same activity should have the same color code. This will help children in choosing take-home kits as even nonreaders tend to remember colors they have chosen.

2. Print the teacher's name and room number on the "Return to" tag. (In case the Learning Totes are left on the school bus or in the cafeteria, etc., this will help get the kit returned to you.)

3. Laminate the tote activity sheet or mount it onto tagboard or cardboard.

4. Follow the directions for each individual skill. Instruct volunteers on how to complete the manipulative components for each kit. Color, laminate, cut, and place finished pieces in the small plastic bag or 6" x 9" (15.24 x 22.86 cm) envelope. Write the name of the Learning Tote on the bag or envelope. (Laminate when possible to make parts last longer. Otherwise use manila tagboard.)

GA1471

5. Place each laminated or mounted tote activity sheet in a large plastic bag. Place any other full-size pages and the bag or envelope containing small pieces into the large seal-top bag *behind* the activity sheet. (The color coded tote activity page should be fully visible.)

6. As an option, place ten to twelve "Tote Notes" in each plastic bag.

7. Organize as many mini workshops as you can early in the school year, and you will have several of each kit ready to circulate in your classroom. When all kits are completed, store them in open file boxes for easy access. You may wish to use bright and attractive Con-Tact™ paper to make the file boxes appealing to students.

8. Now you're ready to start circulating Take-Home Learning Totes!

    • Send the letter of explanation home to parents.

    • A few days after sending the letter, let each child select a Learning Tote. Instruct children to return it the next day. A child that does not return a kit may not take out another one.

    • Use the checkout chart to monitor the return of Learning Totes.

    • Have children file "Tote Notes" in a ballot-type box if you wish to use this optional system. Emphasize that signed "Tote Notes" should not be placed in the Learning Tote plastic bag, but should be returned separately to the ballot-type box. Check the box every week or two. Reward participation as desired. Encourage students who are not participating to take a kit home.

GA1471

Take-Home Learning Tote "Extras"

A few extra management tools are included for you to use at your discretion.

Tote Notes are small slips for recording parent-child accountability. They help you monitor a student's participation, use of skill topics and the activities completed within each skill. Reproduce the page of Tote Notes and include a supply of ten to twelve notes in each kit for parents to sign and return.

Tote Note
Child's Name _____
Title of Learning Tote _____
#'s of Activities Completed _____
Adult's Signature _____
Please put signed note in your child's school bag–not in the plastic Learning Tote bag.

A Blank Take-Home Learning Tote activity sheet is included. Reproduce this page and use it to create your own skill topics. Use a brightly colored marker for lettering the kit, type out the activities and contents and create your own manipulatives.

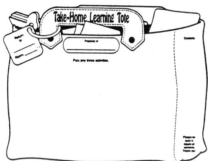

A Checkout Chart is included to keep track of students who have checked out Learning Totes. Simply laminate this chart and use a wax pencil to mark the appropriate square when a student checks out a kit. Erase the wax mark when the kit is returned.

As parents become familiar with the ease of using Learning Totes, your students will be eager to check them out frequently. This combined motivation will give your students added success in learning new skills.

To the Family

Dear Family,

Within a few days your child will be bringing home a new learning program designed for adults like yourself to use easily and successfully with your child. The program is called Take-Home Learning Totes and features a simple family instruction activity sheet and colorful motivating components for you and your child to work with. Each kit will give you choices of activities and will include all the materials you need.

Kits are sent home for overnight use. It is very important that the kit be returned **with all materials** in the seal-top bag the very next school day. Your child will be able to take home another Learning Tote only if the previous one has been returned.

You may notice that your child chooses the same Take-Home Learning Tote on occasion. This is perfectly acceptable. Children learn from repetition and will feel great satisfaction when they are successful doing these activities. There may be a few exercises that are difficult early in the school year. Select activities that your child is capable of doing now. Do the more difficult ones later in the school year.

Please reserve about ten minutes for working with your child whenever a Take-Home Learning Tote is brought home. Choose a quiet place where the time and learning activity are free from distractions and interruptions. It is very likely that you will both look forward to working together when the sessions are limited to about ten minutes.

These activities are supplemental to the classroom program. Your child is not evaluated by activities from the Take-Home Learning Totes. The kits that your child selects and returns are monitored much like a library system so that I know who has a particular kit.

A great deal of time has been spent in the preparation of the Learning Totes. Please supervise the return of all kit pieces and components closely when your child brings the kit back to school. The contents of each kit are clearly listed on the activity sheet so you can be sure everything is returned. Just like a missing piece would ruin a puzzle, a missing component to a kit could make some activities impossible to do. Your help is appreciated.

If you have any comments or questions about working with Take-Home Learning Totes, I would be happy to hear from you.

Sincerely,

To the Teacher:
Use these **Tote Notes** as an optional system to keep track of kits students have used and the activities they have completed within each kit.

Keep a supply of ten to twelve **Tote Notes** in each Learning Tote. Refill as needed.

Tote Note

Child's Name _____

Title of Learning Tote _____

#'s of Activities Completed _____

Adult's Signature _____

Please put signed note in your child's school bag—not in the plastic Learning Tote bag.

Tote Note

Child's Name _____

Title of Learning Tote _____

#'s of Activities Completed _____

Adult's Signature _____

Please put signed note in your child's school bag—not in the plastic Learning Tote bag.

Tote Note

Child's Name _____

Title of Learning Tote _____

#'s of Activities Completed _____

Adult's Signature _____

Please put signed note in your child's school bag—not in the plastic Learning Tote bag.

Tote Note

Child's Name _____

Title of Learning Tote _____

#'s of Activities Completed _____

Adult's Signature _____

Please put signed note in your child's school bag—not in the plastic Learning Tote bag.

Tote Note

Child's Name _____

Title of Learning Tote _____

#'s of Activities Completed _____

Adult's Signature _____

Please put signed note in your child's school bag—not in the plastic Learning Tote bag.

Tote Note

Child's Name _____

Title of Learning Tote _____

#'s of Activities Completed _____

Adult's Signature _____

Please put signed note in your child's school bag—not in the plastic Learning Tote bag.

Tote Note

Child's Name _____

Title of Learning Tote _____

#'s of Activities Completed _____

Adult's Signature _____

Please put signed note in your child's school bag—not in the plastic Learning Tote bag.

Tote Note

Child's Name _____

Title of Learning Tote _____

#'s of Activities Completed _____

Adult's Signature _____

Please put signed note in your child's school bag—not in the plastic Learning Tote bag.

Tote Note

Child's Name _____

Title of Learning Tote _____

#'s of Activities Completed _____

Adult's Signature _____

Please put signed note in your child's school bag—not in the plastic Learning Tote bag.

GA1471

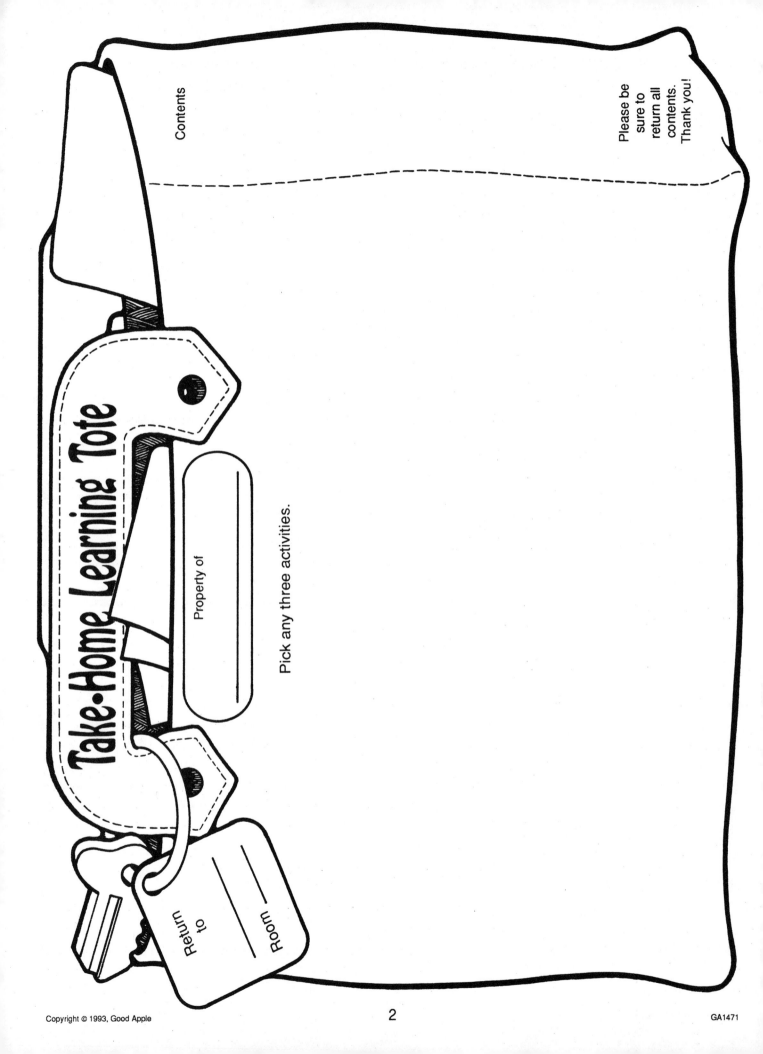

Contents

Please be sure to return all contents. Thank you!

Take-Home Learning Tote

Property of _____

Pick any three activities.

Return to _____

Room _____

2

GA1471

Take-Home Learning Totes
Checkout Chart

Student's Name	Creative Writing	Poetry	Ending Punctuation	Reading Pictures	Multiple Meaning Words	Rhyming Words	Classification	Cause and Effect	Similes	Analogies	Comprehension	Sequencing	Sight Words—Level 1	Sight Words—Level 2	Long and Short Vowels	Initial Blends with r, l	Alphabetical Order	Nouns and Verbs	Contractions	Compound Words	Word Problems	Turnaround Family Math Facts	Place Value	Before, Between and After	Ordinal Numbers	Fractions	Measurement	Money	Graphing and Tallying	Probability with Graphing

Reproduce this page as needed to accommodate all students' names.

GA1471

Take-Home Learning Tote

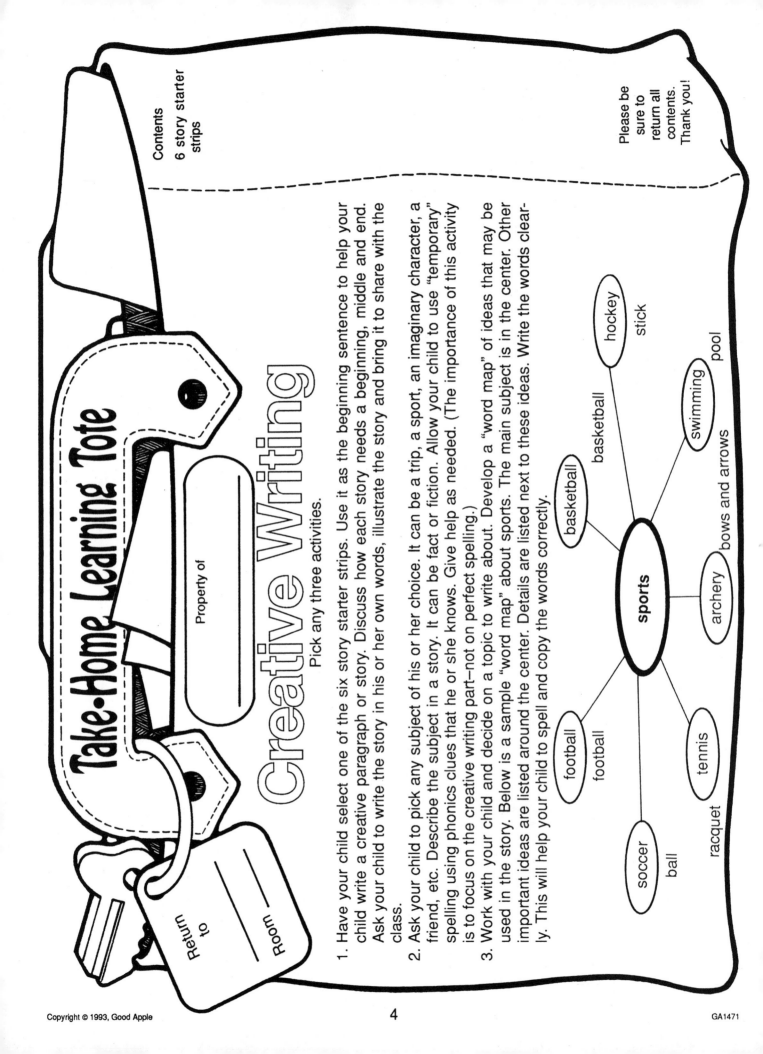

Property of _____

Return to _____

Room _____

Creative Writing

Pick any three activities.

1. Have your child select one of the six story starter strips. Use it as the beginning sentence to help your child write a creative paragraph or story. Discuss how each story needs a beginning, middle and end. Ask your child to write the story in his or her own words, illustrate the story and bring it to share with the class.

2. Ask your child to pick any subject of his or her choice. It can be a trip, a sport, an imaginary character, a friend, etc. Describe the subject in a story. It can be fact or fiction. Allow your child to use "temporary" spelling using phonics clues that he or she knows. Give help as needed. (The importance of this activity is to focus on the creative writing part–not on perfect spelling.)

3. Work with your child and decide on a topic to write about. Develop a "word map" of ideas that may be used in the story. Below is a sample "word map" about sports. The main subject is in the center. Other important ideas are listed around the center. Details are listed next to these ideas. Write the words clearly. This will help your child to spell and copy the words correctly.

- basketball — basketball
- hockey — stick
- swimming — pool
- archery — bows and arrows
- sports
- football — football
- soccer — ball
- tennis — racquet

4

GA1471

I won first place in the contest because I could . . .

Today my dog really made trouble! He . . .

When we went camping . . .

Yesterday I had this big surprise!

The sign said "KEEP OUT!" but I . . .

I had this funny dream . . .

Creative Writing

Directions: Reproduce this page. Laminate and cut apart the six strips.

5

GA1471

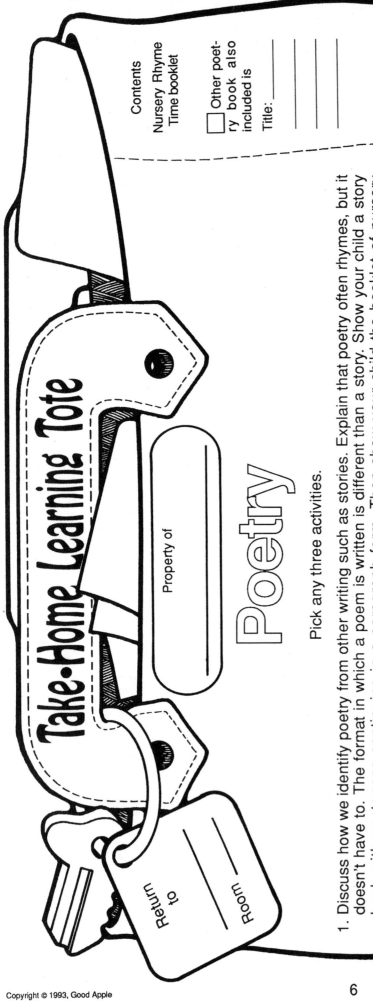

Take-Home Learning Tote

Property of
_____

Return to
_____

Room _____

Poetry

Pick any three activities.

1. Discuss how we identify poetry from other writing such as stories. Explain that poetry often rhymes, but it doesn't have to. The format in which a poem is written is different than a story. Show your child a story book with sentences continuing in a paragraph form. Then show your child the booklet of nursery rhymes. Point out that each one begins with a capital letter because usually each line starts a new sentence.

2. Read the booklet "Nursery Rhyme Time" with your child. Discuss that nursery rhymes are a form of poetry and have rhythm. As you read each poem aloud, use the rhyme to create rhythm. Point out that different poems have different ways of rhyming. Show that in "Humpty Dumpty" every two lines rhyme (wall/fall, men/again). In "Little Jack Horner" the rhyme pattern varies (lines 1 and 2, 3 and 6, and 4 and 5 rhyme). In "Jack and Jill" the rhymes are within the lines (*Jill/hill* in line 1 and *down/crown* in line 3).

3. Help your child write a poem about himself or herself. For example:

   There was a boy named Dave.
   His hair had a permanent wave.
   He liked to play ball
   And that isn't all—
   He was tall and strong and brave.

4. Select a book of poetry you may have at home or visit the library to borrow one. Read different poems aloud. Include some that do not rhyme.

GA1471

Jack and Jill

Jack and Jill went up the hill
To fetch a pail of water;
Jack fell down and broke his crown,
And Jill came tumbling after.

Humpty Dumpty

Humpty Dumpty sat on a wall,
Humpty Dumpty had a great fall.
All the king's horses, and all the king's men,
Couldn't put Humpty together again.

Nursery Rhyme Time

Little Jack Horner

Little Jack Horner
Sat in the corner,
Eating a Christmas pie;
He put in his thumb
And pulled out a plum,
And said, "What a good boy am I!"

Poetry

Directions: Reproduce this page and the following page. Color in the drawings. Cut apart to make an eight-page booklet. Use the Nursery Rhyme Time page for the cover. Arrange the remaining seven pages in any order. Staple the pages together on the left side. You may want to make two to three extra booklets to replace in the tote as booklets become used and worn.

GA1471

Mary, Mary, Quite Contrary

Mary, Mary, quite contrary,
How does your garden grow?
With silver bells, and cockle shells,
And pretty maids all in a row.

Hey, Diddle, Diddle

Hey, diddle, diddle!
The cat and the fiddle,
The cow jumped over the moon;
The little dog laughed
To see such sport,
And the dish ran away with the spoon.

Little Bo-Peep

Little Bo-Peep has lost her sheep,
And can't tell where to find them;
Leave them alone, and they'll come home,
Wagging their tails behind them.

Little Boy Blue

Little Boy Blue, come blow your horn
The sheep's in the meadow, the cow's in the corn.
Where's the little boy who looks after the sheep?
He's under the haystack fast asleep.
Will you wake him? No, not I
For if I do, he'll be sure to cry.

8

GA1471

Contents

6 picture cards

6 sentence strips

6 small punctuation cards

Please be sure to return all contents. Thank you!

Property of _____

Return to _____

Room _____

Ending Punctuation

Pick any three activities.

1. Name the three different punctuation marks and identify them with your child. Discuss when each one is used: the exclamation point (or mark) is used to show excitement, the question mark is used when someone should answer what you ask, and the period is used when you tell something.

2. Ask your child to read the six sentence strips to you. Using these sentences and the six small punctuation cards, ask your child to put the correct punctuation mark at the end of each sentence. Check for accuracy. Review any that are not correct.

3. Mix the punctuation cards and turn them facedown. Pick one. Show it to your child and have him or her make up a sentence that would use that punctuation mark. Let your child select a card and show you the punctuation mark. You make up a sentence. For extra practice, mix the cards and try again.

4. Ask your child to read the sentence on each picture card. Pick a punctuation mark to end each sentence. Place it in the square in the lower right corner. Check for accuracy. Review any that are not correct.

5. Mix the punctuation cards and the picture cards. Pick one of each. Cover the sentence on the picture card. Have your child make up a new sentence about the picture using the punctuation mark picked.

6. Help your child to write a paragraph about going on a picnic. At the end of each sentence, ask what kind of punctuation is needed. Encourage the use of sentences that require exclamation points and question marks.

GA1471

.	.	!	!	?	?

What did you pack for lunch

The teacher said it was time for lunch

It was exciting to see the dog jump

Todd and Susan play on the same team

The roller coaster went so fast

Can you play at my house today

Ending Punctuation

Directions: Reproduce this page. Laminate and cut apart the six picture cards and six individual punctuation marks.

10

When can we go to the zoo

I couldn't wait to go

This book is mine

It's so hot outside

My father likes to cook

What is your dog's name

11

GA1471

Ending Punctuation

Directions: Reproduce this page. Laminate and cut apart the six sentence strips.

Take-Home Learning Tote

Contents

6 picture cards
6 descriptive sentences for picture cards

Please be sure to return all contents. Thank you!

Property of _____

Return to _____

Room _____

Reading Pictures

Pick any three activities.

1. Using the six pictures and sentences, ask your child to look at each picture carefully. Place the sentence that best describes each picture below it. Encourage your child to look for picture clues. Have your child read each sentence aloud.

2. Using the picture cards, ask your child to write his or her own sentence for each picture. Have your child read each sentence to you.

3. Select a picture book to read to your child. Choose any picture in the book. Ask your child to find a sentence on that page that best describes the illustration. Do this for several of the pictures in the book.

4. Look at any illustration in a picture book. Without reading the book, ask your child to write a list of words that describe the picture. Encourage your child to use his or her own phonics skills for spelling. Give help when needed. Write one or two sentences using the list of descriptive words your child wrote. Read the book. Find sentences in the story that may be similar to your child's sentences.

5. Let your child select four pictures to cut out from a magazine. Glue these pictures close to the top of a piece of paper. Leave room below each picture for a sentence. Ask your child to write a sentence about each picture. You can make a reading picture matching activity by cutting off the sentences and then having your child match the sentences to the correct pictures.

6. Rebus sentences use pictures in place of some words. Write and draw to make some rebus sentences for your child to read.

The warm [sun] helped the [flower] grow.

12

GA1471

Eric liked to climb on the monkey bars.

The boys watch their favorite cartoons on videotape.

The monkey and the lion were best friends.

Mom videotaped the soccer game.

The monkey could swing from the tree.

Jason and Kirk like to play video games.

Reading Pictures

Directions: Reproduce this page. Color the illustrations. Laminate and cut apart to yield six picture cards and six sentence cards.

13

GA1471

Take-Home Learning Tote

Property of
_____

Return
to
_____

Room
_____

Multiple Meaning Words

Pick any three activities.

1. Explain to your child that some words can have the same spelling and be pronounced the same way but have more than one meaning. Such words are called *homographs*. An example is:
   The player hit the baseball with a *bat*.
   On Halloween night we may see a witch, a ghost and a *bat*.
   Ask your child if he or she can think of two different meanings for the words *sink*, *trunk* or *nail*.

2. Using the six multiple meaning word cards, ask your child to pick one and act out or tell you two different meanings for each word. Give help if needed.

3. Look at the picture cards. Ask your child to read each sentence and use a word card to fill in the appropriate answer. After choosing the appropriate answers, have your child make up a sentence for each word to show the other meaning.

4. Use the definition cards and the word cards. Ask your child to read the cards and match them correctly to show which two definitions fit each multiple meaning word.

5. Read selections from the charming Amelia Bedelia books by Peggy Parish. Find examples of multiple meanings that cause misunderstandings. Ask your child to tell you what Amelia Bedelia should have done instead of what she did.

GA1471

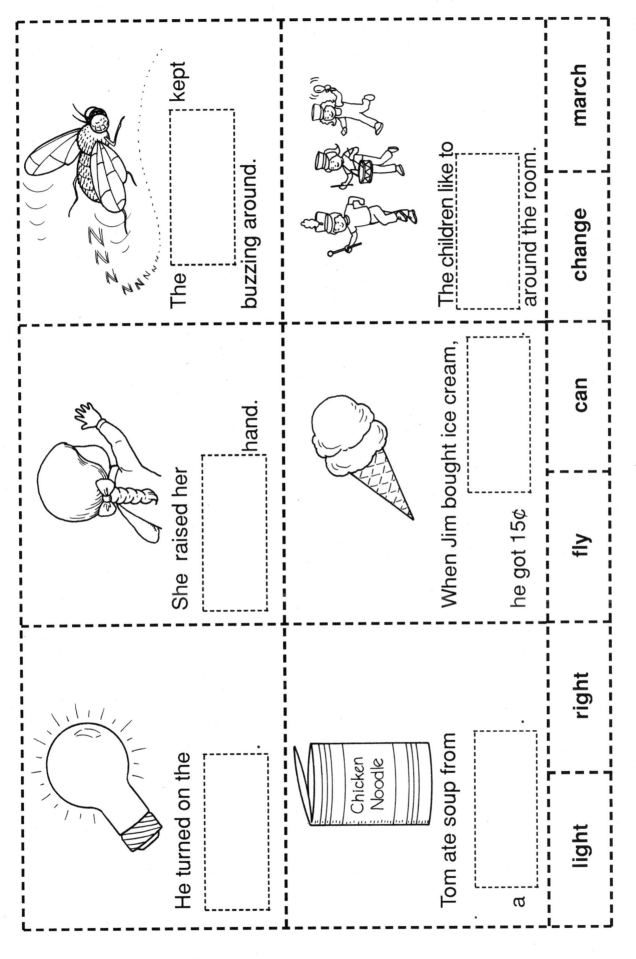

The _____ kept buzzing around.

The children like to _____ around the room.

She raised her _____ hand.

When Jim bought ice cream, he got 15¢ _____

He turned on the _____

Tom ate soup from a _____.

march

change

can

fly

right

light

Multiple Meaning Words

Directions: Reproduce this page. Color the illustrations. Cut apart into six picture cards and six word cards.

15

GA1471

move through the air using wings	to be able to	true, correct, suitable	to walk in step in a group
of little weight, not heavy	a container, usually metal	to alter	third month in the year
brightness	an insect	coins	direction, opposite of left

GA1471

Directions: Reproduce this page. Laminate and cut apart to yield twelve definition cards.

Take-Home Learning Tote

Property of _____

Contents

40 word cards
40 picture cards

Please be
sure to
return all
contents.
Thank you!

Rhyming Words

Pick any three activities.

1. Ask your child to sort the word cards into rhyming families. Point out that *most* rhyming words have the same ending. Words like *chair* and *bear* rhyme but have different endings.

2. Pick one rhyming family. Help your child make up a poem using as many of the words in the rhyming family as possible. You may use rhyming words in addition to those on the word cards. For example:

    The tan man ran to get a fan.
    The tan man ran to get a pan.
    The tan man ran and ran and ran
    To his new tan van.

    Try this two to three times to create different rhymes.

3. Turn the picture cards facedown. Ask your child to pick one and name it. Name three more words that rhyme with the word. Pick again. Repeat several times. Do this same activity using the word cards.

4. This game is similar to the old card game Fish. Shuffle all the rhyming picture cards in a deck. Deal four cards to your child and four to yourself. Each one removes any rhyming pairs from the four cards. If there are three rhyming cards, remove only two! Cards must be removed in pairs. Place all rhyming pairs in front of you so that both of you can see the cards. Look at the remaining cards in your hand and ask your child if he or she has a match to one of your cards. If so, the card must be given to you. If not, you may pick one card from the deck. If you get a match when you draw, remove the pair and you get to ask for another card. If not, it is your child's turn. The winner is the one with the most matches when the cards in the deck are used up.

GA1471

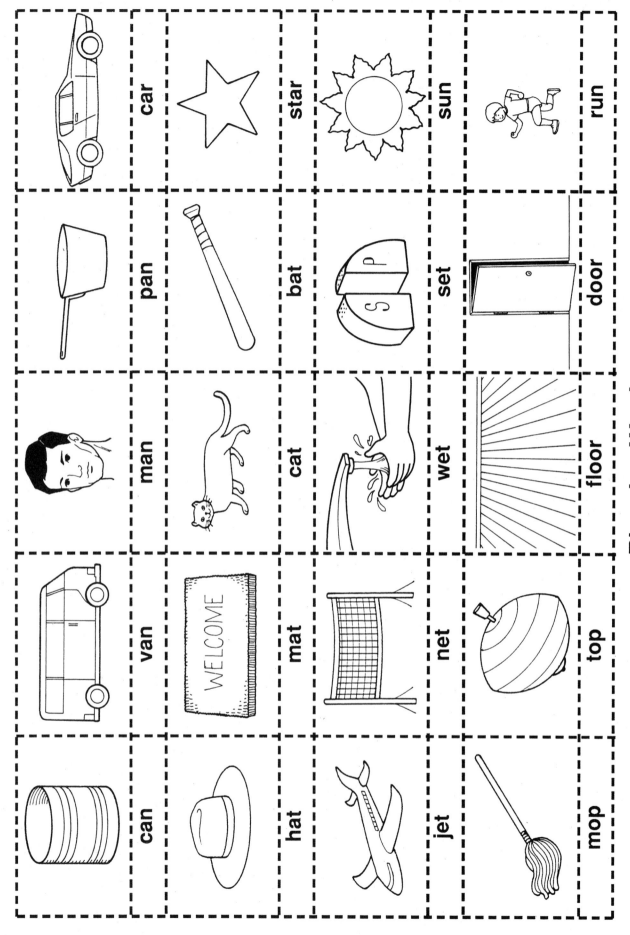

car	star	sun	run	
pan	bat	set	door	
man	cat	wet	floor	
van	mat	net	top	
can	hat	jet	mop	

Rhyming Words

Directions: Reproduce this page and the following page. Laminate and cut cards apart to yield forty picture cards and forty individual word cards.

18

GA1471

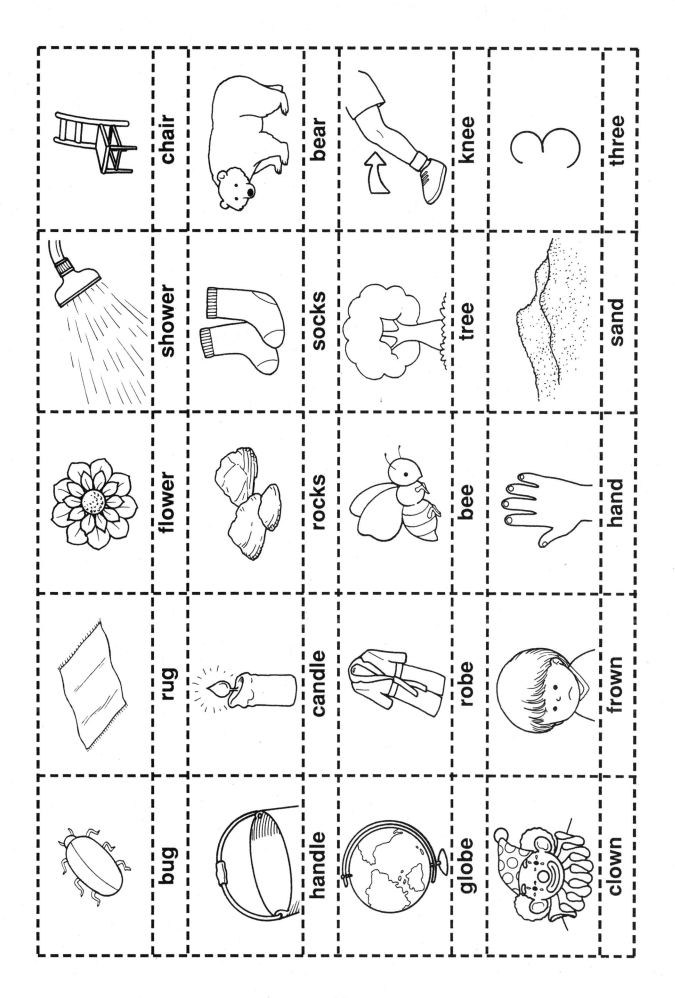

chair

bear

knee

three

shower

socks

tree

sand

flower

rocks

bee

hand

rug

candle

robe

frown

bug

handle

globe

clown

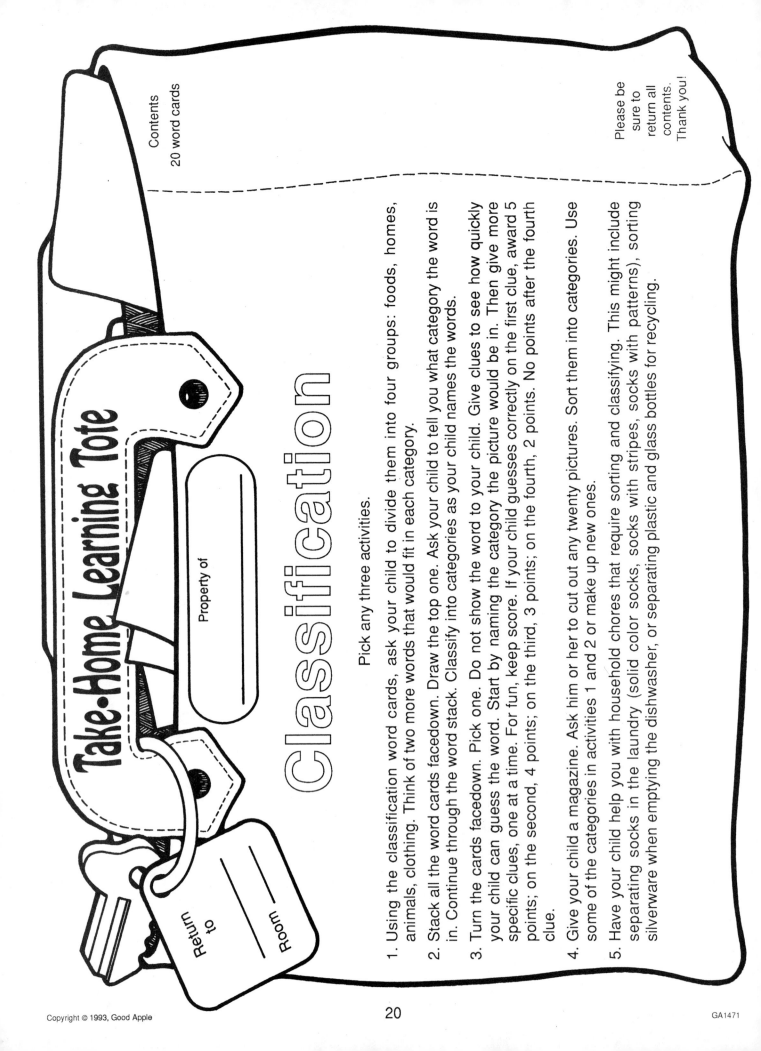

Take-Home Learning Tote

Contents
20 word cards

Property of
_____

Return
to
_____

Room
_____

Please be
sure to
return all
contents.
Thank you!

Classification

Pick any three activities.

1. Using the classification word cards, ask your child to divide them into four groups: foods, homes, animals, clothing. Think of two more words that would fit in each category.

2. Stack all the word cards facedown. Draw the top one. Ask your child to tell you what category the word is in. Continue through the word stack. Classify into categories as your child names the words.

3. Turn the cards facedown. Pick one. Do not show the word to your child. Give clues to see how quickly your child can guess the word. Start by naming the category the picture would be in. Then give more specific clues, one at a time. For fun, keep score. If your child guesses correctly on the first clue, award 5 points; on the second, 4 points; on the third, 3 points; on the fourth, 2 points. No points after the fourth clue.

4. Give your child a magazine. Ask him or her to cut out any twenty pictures. Sort them into categories. Use some of the categories in activities 1 and 2 or make up new ones.

5. Have your child help you with household chores that require sorting and classifying. This might include separating socks in the laundry (solid color socks, socks with stripes, socks with patterns), sorting silverware when emptying the dishwasher, or separating plastic and glass bottles for recycling.

20

GA1471

coat	horse	tent	soup
dress	cow	house	bread
shirt	pig	igloo	meat
socks	duck	nest	eggs
shorts	dog	barn	cereal

Classification

Directions: Reproduce this page. Laminate and cut apart to yield twenty word cards.

GA1471

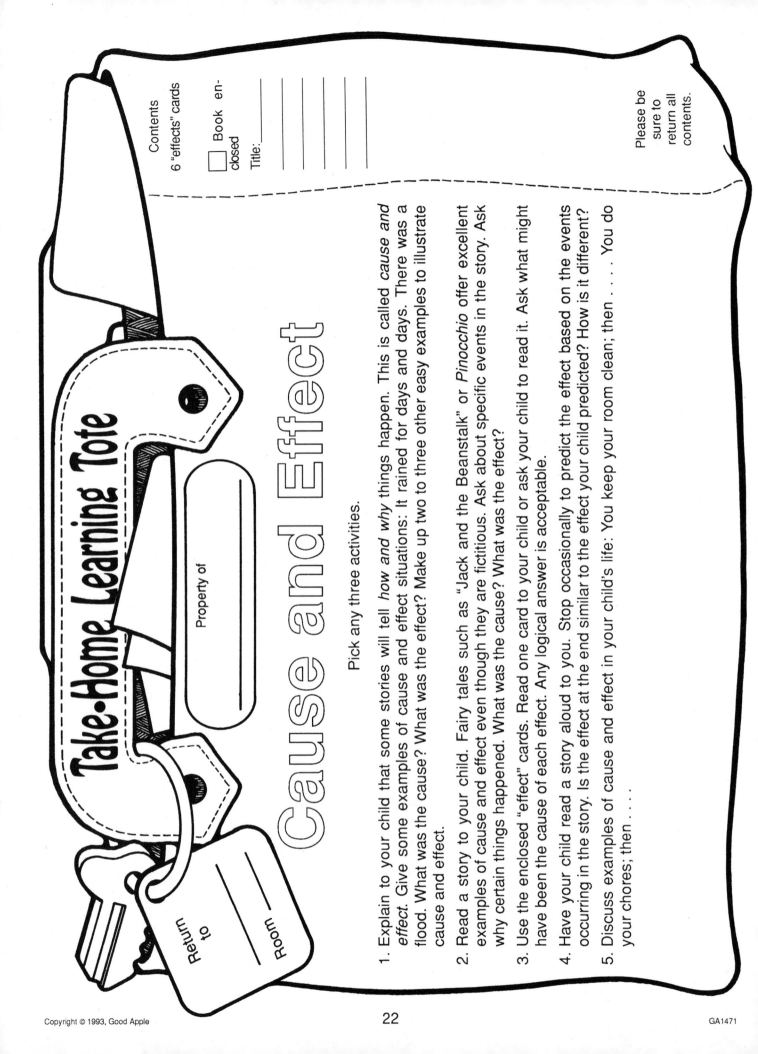

Take-Home Learning Tote

Contents
6 "effects" cards
☐ Book enclosed
Title: _____

Please be sure to return all contents.

Property of _____

Return to _____ Room

Cause and Effect

Pick any three activities.

1. Explain to your child that some stories will tell *how and why* things happen. This is called *cause and effect*. Give some examples of cause and effect situations: It rained for days and days. There was a flood. What was the cause? What was the effect? Make up two to three other easy examples to illustrate cause and effect.

2. Read a story to your child. Fairy tales such as "Jack and the Beanstalk" or *Pinocchio* offer excellent examples of cause and effect even though they are fictitious. Ask about specific events in the story. Ask why certain things happened. What was the cause? What was the effect?

3. Use the enclosed "effect" cards. Read one card to your child or ask your child to read it. Ask what might have been the cause of each effect. Any logical answer is acceptable.

4. Have your child read a story aloud to you. Stop occasionally to predict the effect based on the events occurring in the story. Is the effect at the end similar to the effect your child predicted? How is it different?

5. Discuss examples of cause and effect in your child's life: You keep your room clean; then . . . . You do your chores; then . . . .

GA1471

The ambulance was rushing down the road.

Laura was happy to see her dad at last.

The Bluejays team won first place.

Jeff was dizzy after he left the amusement park.

David got all A's on his report card.

The garden was full of beautiful flowers.

Cause and Effect

Directions: Reproduce this page. Color the illustrations. Laminate and cut apart the six cards.

23

GA1471

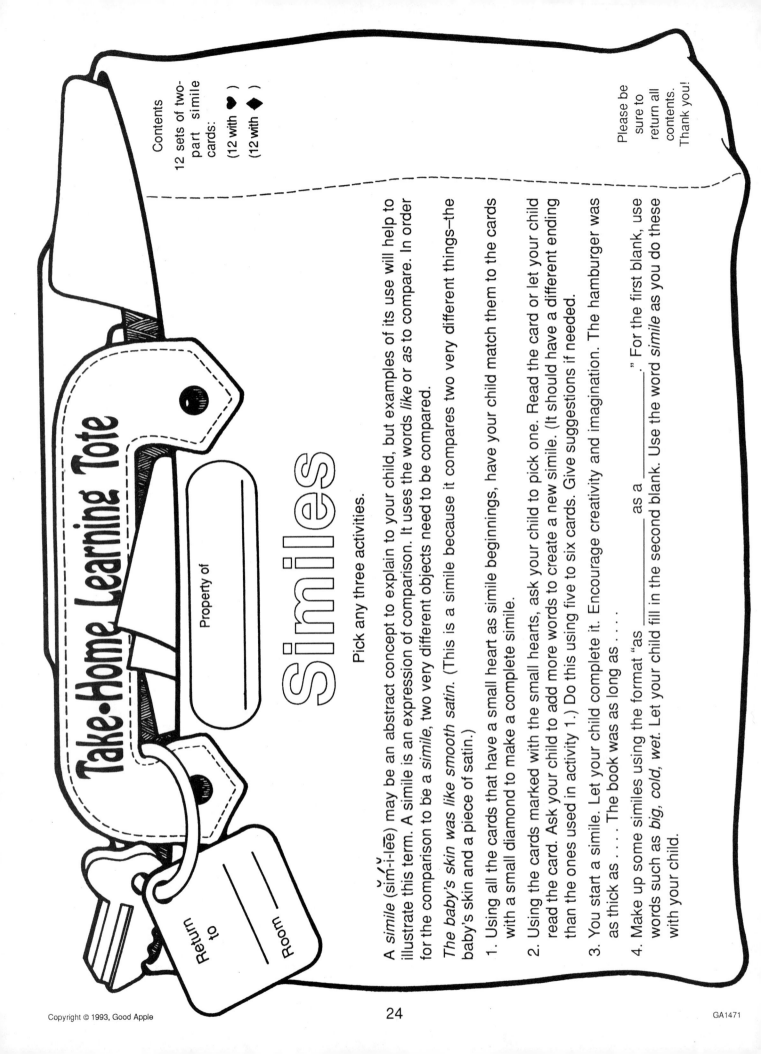

Take-Home Learning Tote

Property of
_____

Return to
_____

Room
_____

Contents
12 sets of two-part simile cards:
(12 with ❤)
(12 with ◆)

Please be sure to return all contents. Thank you!

Similes

Pick any three activities.

A *simile* (sĭm-i-lē) may be an abstract concept to explain to your child, but examples of its use will help to illustrate this term. A simile is an expression of comparison. It uses the words *like* or *as* to compare. In order for the comparison to be a *simile*, two very different objects need to be compared.

The baby's skin was like smooth satin. (This is a simile because it compares two very different things—the baby's skin and a piece of satin.)

1. Using all the cards that have a small heart as simile beginnings, have your child match them to the cards with a small diamond to make a complete simile.

2. Using the cards marked with the small hearts, ask your child to pick one. Read the card or let your child read the card. Ask your child to add more words to create a new simile. (It should have a different ending than the ones used in activity 1.) Do this using five to six cards. Give suggestions if needed.

3. You start a simile. Let your child complete it. Encourage creativity and imagination. The hamburger was as thick as . . . . The book was as long as . . . .

4. Make up some similes using the format "as _____ as a _____." For the first blank, use words such as *big, cold, wet*. Let your child fill in the second blank. Use the word *simile* as you do these with your child.

24

GA1471

♦ honey pot.

♦ vegetable garden.

♦ house.

♦ needles and pins.

♦ mirror.

♦ taking a warm shower.

● The glue was as sticky as a

● The grass smelled as fresh as a

● The elephant was as big as a

● The thorns were as sharp as

● The new shoes were as shiny as a

● Playing in the rain was like

Similes

Directions: Reproduce this page and the following page. Laminate and cut apart to yield twelve sets of two-part simile cards.

◆ soft, white teddy bear.

◆ big, red apple.

◆ star at night.

◆ thick, white cotton.

◆ tree.

◆ big, silver bird.

♥ The clouds looked like a

♥ The balloon looked like a

♥ The diamond was shining like a

♥ The snow was as soft as

♥ The man was as tall as a

♥ The airplane looked like a

26

Take-Home Learning Tote

Property of _____

Return to _____

Room _____

Contents

4 sentence strips

28 word cards

Please be sure to return all contents. Thank you!

Analogies

Pick any three activities.

These activities involve making analogies. Your child will learn to see likenesses, comparisons and similarities between two pairs of items. A sample of an analogy is: *Library is to books as museum is to paintings.*

1. Using the word cards and sentence strips, ask your child to read each sentence. Ask your child to pick the word card that best fits the sentence. Remind your child to listen to the whole sentence before choosing an answer. Give help as needed.

2. Using the word cards, make *relationship pairs.* You make the first pair; then ask your child to make a similar pair. You might choose the words *cow* and *milk.* Discuss the relationship between cow and milk. Ask your child to find a similar pair of relationship cards. A correct choice would be *chicken* and *egg.* Do this several times.

3. Sort out the word cards with an * on them. Ask your child to pick one card and read it to you. Using the word, make up an analogy for your child to complete. For example: If your child picks the word *cold,* you might say "Cold is to winter as hot is to . . . ." Do this several times to make up different analogies.

4. Ask your child to complete these analogies: Neck is to giraffe as trunk is to . . . . .

   Scale is to weigh as ruler is to . . . .

   Food is to hungry as drink is to . . . .

   Refrigerator is to food as closet is to . . . .

   School is to learn as church is to . . . . .

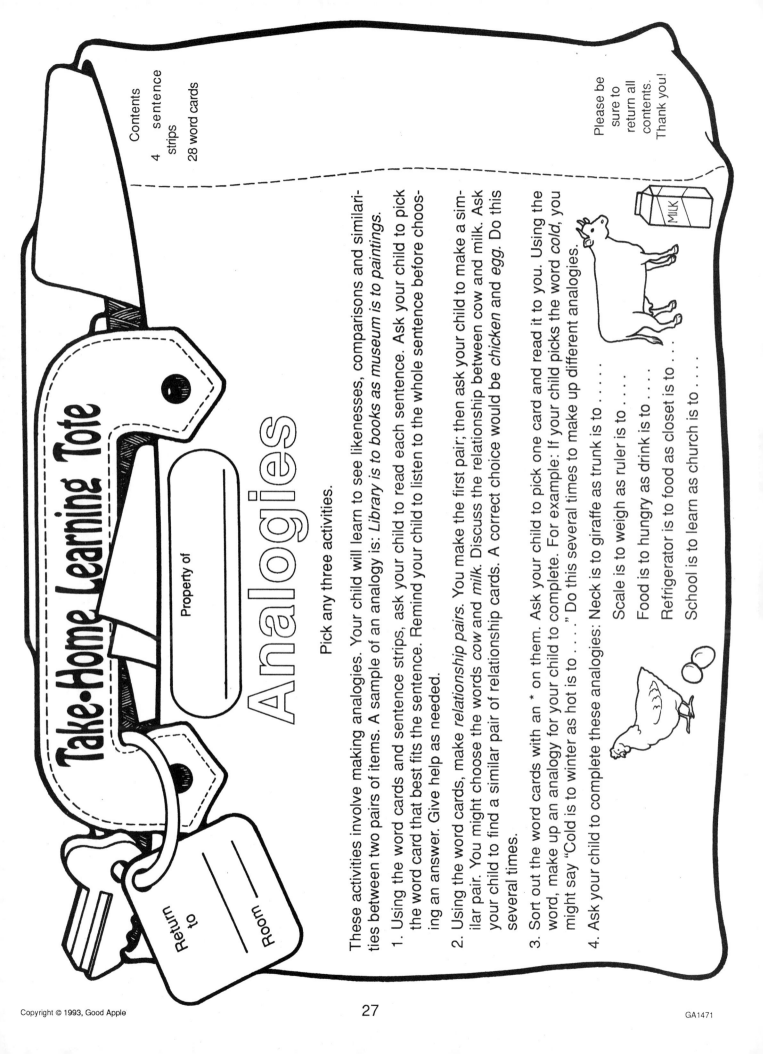

GA1471

sweet	warm	see	night
Sugar is to	Sun is to	A picture is to	Dark is to
as a lemon is to	as snow is to	as a song is to	as light is to

28

Analogies

Directions: Reproduce this page and the following page. Laminate and cut apart the four sentence strips

hear	song	see*	picture
cold*	snow*	warm	sun*
table	tablecloth	floor	carpet
cat*	meow	dog*	bark
sour	lemon	sweet	sugar
egg	chicken*	milk	cow*
day*	light	night*	dark

Directions: Reproduce this page. Laminate and cut apart to yield twenty-eight cards.

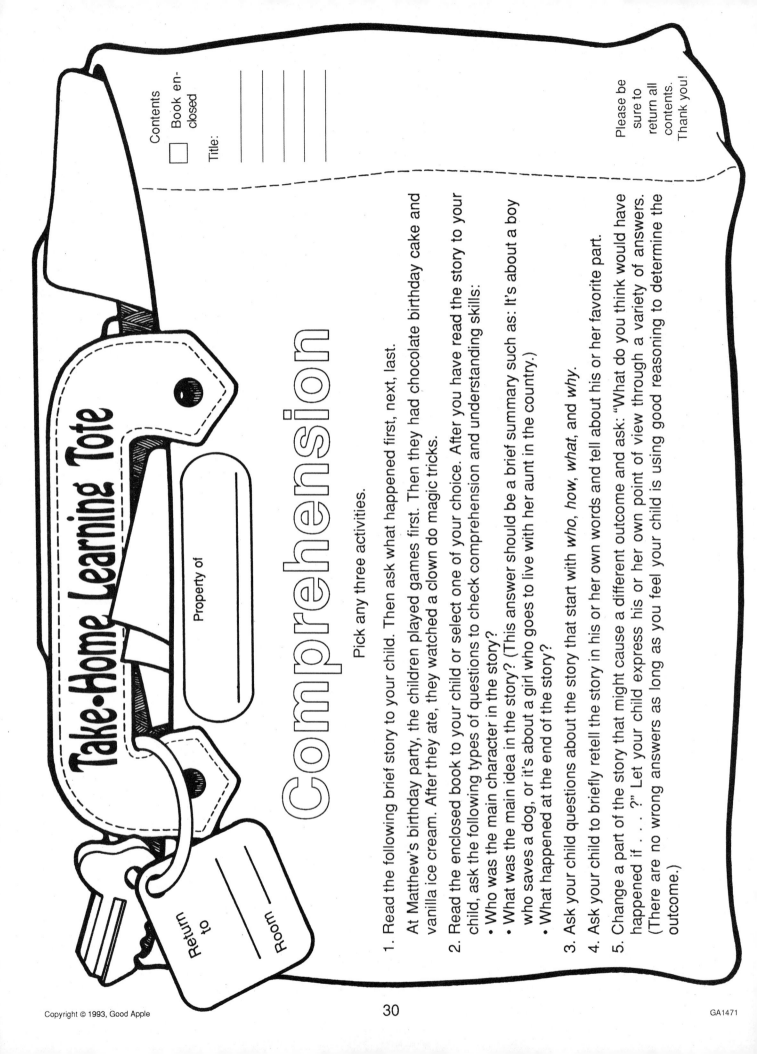

Property of

Return to _____
Room _____

Contents
☐ Book enclosed
Title: _____

Please be sure to return all contents. Thank you!

Comprehension

Pick any three activities.

1. Read the following brief story to your child. Then ask what happened first, next, last.

   At Matthew's birthday party, the children played games first. Then they had chocolate birthday cake and vanilla ice cream. After they ate, they watched a clown do magic tricks.

2. Read the enclosed book to your child or select one of your choice. After you have read the story to your child, ask the following types of questions to check comprehension and understanding skills:
   • Who was the main character in the story?
   • What was the main idea in the story? (This answer should be a brief summary such as: It's about a boy who saves a dog, or it's about a girl who goes to live with her aunt in the country.)
   • What happened at the end of the story?

3. Ask your child questions about the story that start with *who, how, what,* and *why.*

4. Ask your child to briefly retell the story in his or her own words and tell about his or her favorite part.

5. Change a part of the story that might cause a different outcome and ask: "What do you think would have happened if . . . ?" Let your child express his or her own point of view through a variety of answers. (There are no wrong answers as long as you feel your child is using good reasoning to determine the outcome.)

30

GA1471

Take-Home Learning Tote

Property of

Return to

Room

Sequencing

Pick any three activities.

1. Using picture clues, ask your child to sort all pictures into stories. Look for the same characters or items in the pictures. Arrange each story in sequential order.

2. Pick out one sequence story. Ask your child to tell the story as he or she places the pictures in correct order. Ask questions like "Why did this picture have to happen first? Could this picture happen before this picture? Why?"

3. Pick out another sequence story. Mix the cards. Ask your child to arrange the pictures in sequential order and tell you the story. Remove all pictures except one. Ask your child to tell you what happened *immediately before* and *immediately after* that picture.

4. Using cards 1-4 for four-part stories and 1-5 for five-part stories, ask your child to place the numbers in order in a horizontal row. Place the story pictures, one story at a time, in order under the correct numbers.

5. Read the following story to your child. Ask your child to identify the words that help tell the order of events in the story (first, next, at last).

   Kristi was in a hurry to get ready for school. First she put on her favorite outfit with the matching bow for her hair. Next, she went downstairs to eat breakfast. At last, it was time for the bus, so Kristi ran to the bus stop to meet her friends.

   After reading the story to your child, ask to have the story repeated to you. Check to see that the events were repeated in correct order. Make up other similar stories with three to five events using the words *first, then, next,* and *last.* Ask your child to repeat the sequence of events.

Contents

2 four-panel stories

2 five-panel stories

number cards 1-5

Please be sure to return all contents. Thank you!

31

GA1471

Sequencing

Directions: Reproduce this page and the following page. Color the illustrations. Laminate and cut out the individual panels of each of the four stories. Cut out the five number cards.

GA1471

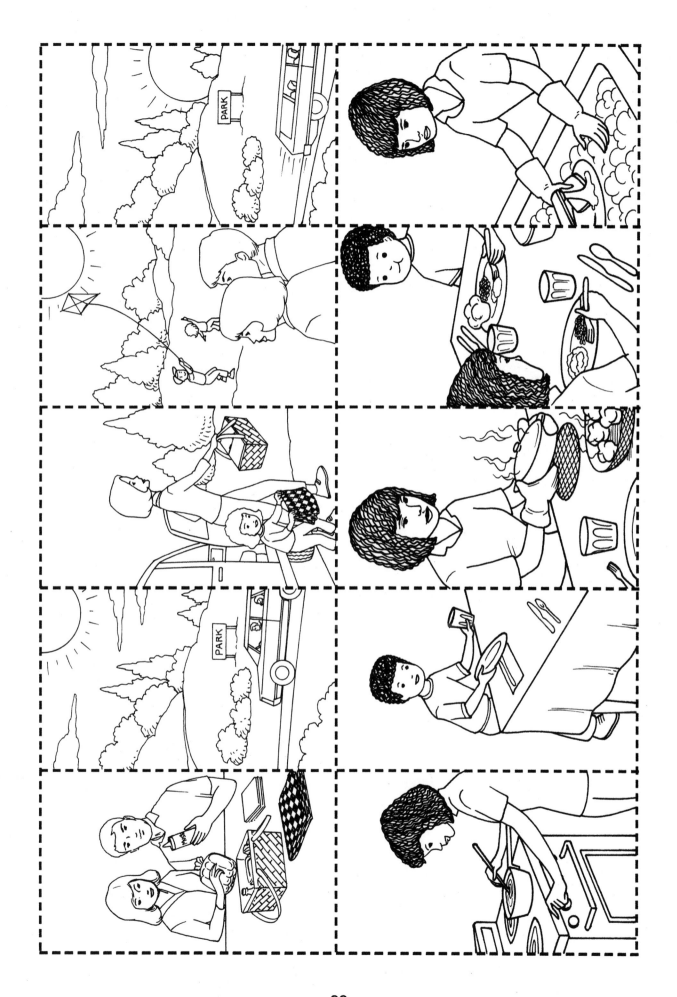

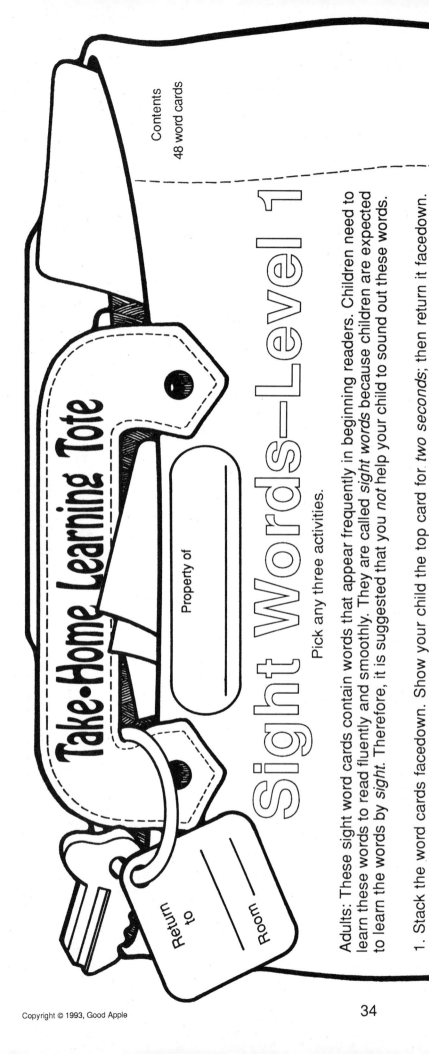

Take-Home Learning Tote

Property of
_____

Return
to
_____

Room _____

Contents
48 word cards

Please be
sure to
return all
contents.
Thank you!

Sight Words—Level 1

Pick any three activities.

Adults: These sight word cards contain words that appear frequently in beginning readers. Children need to learn these words to read fluently and smoothly. They are called *sight words* because children are expected to learn the words *by sight*. Therefore, it is suggested that you *not* help your child to sound out these words.

1. Stack the word cards facedown. Show your child the top card for *two seconds*; then return it facedown. Ask your child to say the word. If the response is correct, give your child the card. If incorrect, return it to the bottom of the stack. After going through the deck twice, ask your child to count the cards in his or her stack to see how many correct responses there were. Use the remaining stack for more practice. If your child cannot identify the word, say the word and have your child repeat it.

2. Select five to six words that form a sentence. Place the words in scrambled order. Ask your child to rearrange the words to make a sentence. Repeat three to four times using different words.

3. *Each card has a small numeral (1, 2 or 3) in the upper left corner. These are used for scoring in this game.* Spread out all cards, facedown, on the table. Ask your child to pick a card, name the word, and write down the score if the response was correct. (There is no score for an incorrect word or a word not identified.) Select ten words. Add up the scores. Try another set of ten words. Compare the scores. Discuss why the scores could be different even if all ten words were identified correctly both times!

4. Ask your child to make sentences with the word cards. Help your child to pick out *action words* (verbs) such as *come, jumps, looks, run,* etc., which are needed in every sentence.

5. Sort word cards by beginning letter. Arrange in stacks; then read each stack. Set aside those stacks where your child knows all the words. Review remaining word stacks.

34

GA1471

and ¹	**boy** ¹	**down** ¹	**here** ¹
away ²	**can** ²	**find** ²	**house** ²
ball ³	**cannot** ³	**funny** ³	**in** ³
big ¹	**cat** ¹	**girl** ¹	**is** ¹
blue ²	**come** ²	**go** ²	**it** ²
boat ³	**dog** ³	**help** ³	**jump** ³

Sight Words

Directions: Reproduce this page and the following page. Laminate and cut cards apart to yield forty-eight cards.

35

1 to	2 two	3 up	1 we	2 where	3 you
1 play	2 run	3 said	1 see	2 the	3 three
1 make	2 makes	3 me	1 my	2 not	3 one
1 jumps	2 jumping	3 little	1 look	2 looks	3 looking

36

GA1471

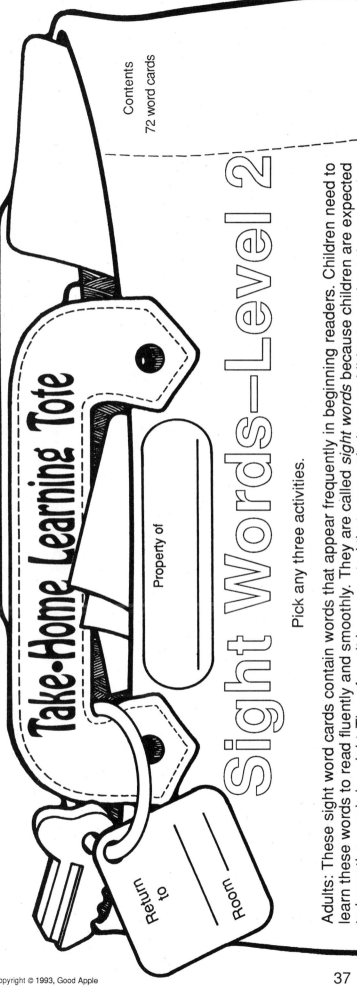

Take-Home Learning Tote

Property of

Return to _____

Room _____

Contents
72 word cards

Please be sure to return all contents. Thank you!

Sight Words—Level 2

Pick any three activities.

Adults: These sight word cards contain words that appear frequently in beginning readers. Children need to learn these words to read fluently and smoothly. They are called *sight words* because children are expected to learn the words by *sight*. Therefore, it is suggested that you *not* help your child to sound out these words.

1. Stack the word cards facedown. Show your child the top card for *two seconds*; then return it facedown. Ask your child to say the word. If the response is correct, give the child the card. If incorrect, return it to the bottom of the stack. After going through the deck twice, ask your child to count the cards in his or her stack to see how many correct responses there were. Use the remaining stack for more practice. If your child cannot identify the word, say the word and have your child repeat it.

2. Select five to six words that form a sentence. Place the words in scrambled order. Ask your child to rearrange the words to make a sentence. Repeat three to four times using different words.

3. *Each card has a small numeral (1, 2 or 3) in the upper left corner. These are used for scoring in this game.* Spread out all cards, facedown, on the table. Ask your child to pick a card, name the word, and write down the score if the response was correct. (There is no score for an incorrect word or a word not identified.) Select ten words. Add up the scores. Try another set of ten words. Compare the scores. Discuss why the scores could be different even if all ten words were identified correctly both times!

4. Ask your child to make sentences with the word cards. Help your child to pick out *action words* (verbs) such as *came, eat, likes, saw*, etc., which are needed in every sentence.

5. Sort word cards by beginning letter. Arrange in stacks; then read each stack. Set aside those stacks where your child knows all the words. Review remaining word stacks.

37

GA1471

1 eats	1 cars	1 black	1 all
2 eating	2 children	2 box	2 are
3 father	3 did	3 brown	3 at
1 four	1 do	1 but	1 ate
2 get	2 doll	2 came	2 baby
3 good	3 eat	3 car	3 be

Sight Words

Directions: Reproduce this page and the following two pages. Laminate and cut cards apart to yield seventy-two cards.

GA1471

1 pretty

2 ran

3 ride

1 rides

2 saw

3 say

1 no

2 now

3 on

1 our

2 out

3 please

1 like

2 likes

3 man

1 mother

2 must

3 new

1 hat

2 hats

3 have

1 he

2 ice cream

3 into

GA1471

1 what	2 white	3 who	1 will	2 with	3 yes
1 under	2 want	3 wants	1 was	2 well	3 went
1 there	2 they	3 this	1 too	2 toy	3 truck
1 she	2 snowman	3 so	1 soon	2 sun	3 that

GA1471

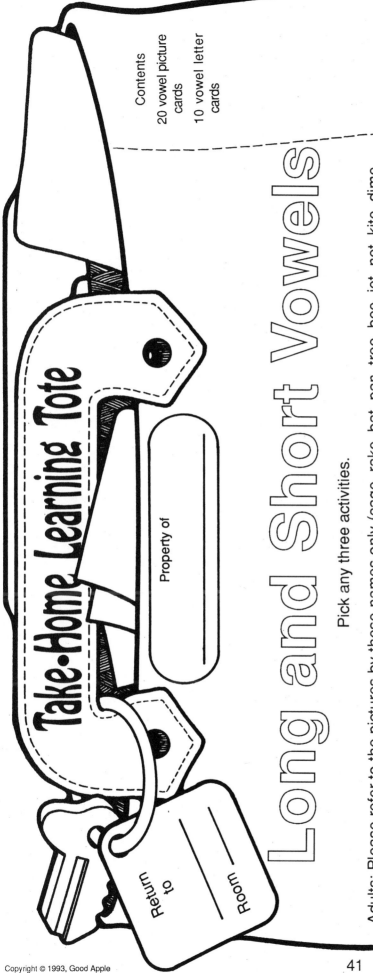

Contents

20 vowel picture cards

10 vowel letter cards

Please be sure to return all contents. Thank you!

Long and Short Vowels

Pick any three activities.

Adults: Please refer to the pictures by these names only (cage, rake, bat, pan, tree, bee, jet, net, kite, dime, pin, wig, boat, home, pot, log, bugle, unicorn, bug, sun).

1. Ask your child to sort the pictures according to long and short vowel sounds. (You will hear the letter name in each **long** vowel sound—**ā** as in *cage* and **ē** as in *be*, etc.)

2. Using only the long vowel pictures and long vowel letter cards (a, e, i, o, u), ask your child to sort the pictures into five groups according to each vowel sound. Then match the vowel letter cards to the correct group of vowel picture cards.

3. Repeat activity 2 for short vowel sounds.

4. Turn all the vowel picture cards facedown in rows. Ask your child to turn up two pictures at a time trying to make a vowel sound match. When a correct match is made, remove those two cards from the game. Cards that do not match are turned facedown. Try again. Continue until all matches are made.

5. Put the picture cards in a paper bag. Ask your child to take out one card, name the vowel and tell whether it is a long or short sound.

6. Put the following picture cards in a paper bag: Ask your child to take out one card. Say the name of the picture. Can he or she think of another word that has the same vowel sound? (If the *cage* card is drawn, your child may say any word with a long **ā** sound such as *cāke*, *lāne*, *dāy*, etc.)

GA1471

Long and Short Vowels

Directions: Reproduce this page. Color the illustrations. Laminate and cut apart to yield twenty cards.

42

GA1471

ū

ŭ

ō

ŏ

ī

ĭ

ē

ĕ

ā

ă

Directions: Reproduce this page. Laminate and cut cards apart.

GA1471

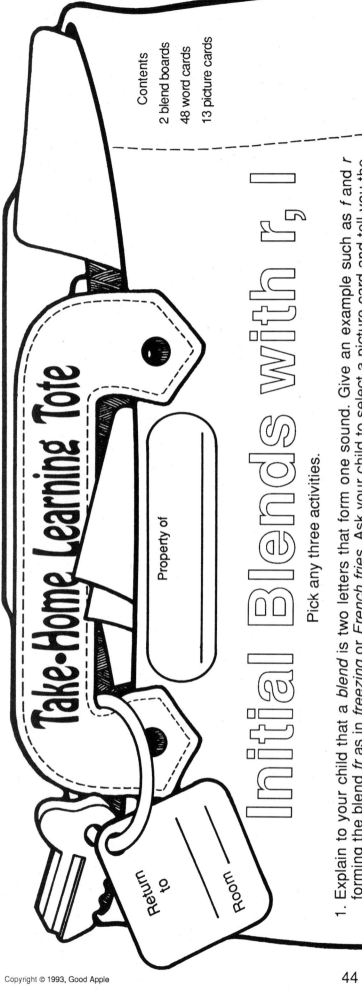

Take-Home Learning Tote

Property of _____

Return
to _____

Room _____

Initial Blends with r, l

Pick any three activities.

1. Explain to your child that a *blend* is two letters that form one sound. Give an example such as *f* and *r* forming the blend *fr* as in *freezing* or *French fries*. Ask your child to select a picture card and tell you the blend he or she hears. (Your child should say the two-letter sound such as *gr* or *cl* and not name the letters *g* and *r* or *c* and *l*.) Go over any incorrect responses.

2. Use the blending boards. Ask your child to place the picture cards in the correct blocks on the boards. After all picture cards are sorted, have your child say the picture names to hear the blends.

3. Put ten word cards in a stack. Hold these cards in your hand so that your child cannot see the words. Ask your child to number a piece of paper vertically from 1-10. Read the first word. Have your child write the two-letter blend heard at the beginning of the word next to 1 on the paper. As you call a word, return the card to the bottom of your stack so that the cards stay in the same order as you called them. This will help when you check your child's responses. Call all ten words. Check the responses. Review errors. Select ten new word cards for further practice.

4. Place all word cards faceup. Give your child clues to one of the words (for example, a lady that is getting married is called a _____). Have your child name the word to fill the blank; then find the word card and say the blend. Give clues for five to six words.

5. Point to any blend on the blend board. Ask your child to think of words that start with that blend. These can be *any* words your child knows—in addition to the words on the cards.

6. Match word cards to the corresponding block on the blend board. Say the words in each block to hear how the blends are alike.

44

GA1471

br	gr
cr	pr
dr	tr
fr	

Initial Blends

Directions: Reproduce this page and the following page to make two "blend boards." Laminate each board and attach to sturdy cardboard backing. DO NOT CUT INDIVIDUAL CARDS APART.

GA1471

bl	cl	fl
gl	pl	sl

GA1471

Directions: Reproduce this page. Color the illustrations. Laminate and cut cards apart to yield thirteen picture cards.

47

black	flower	plump	brown	crown	drapes
clip	glade	slip	cracker	drive	fruit
flag	plan	bloom	drop	free	grapes
glad	slate	climb	frog	great	propeller
plate	blimp	flood	gravy	pride	truck
sled	down	glove	pretty	train	broom
blue	fly	plant	tree	bride	crunch
clap	gleam	slide	brave	cry	drip

Directions: Reproduce this page. Laminate and cut word cards apart to yield forty-eight cards.

48

GA1471

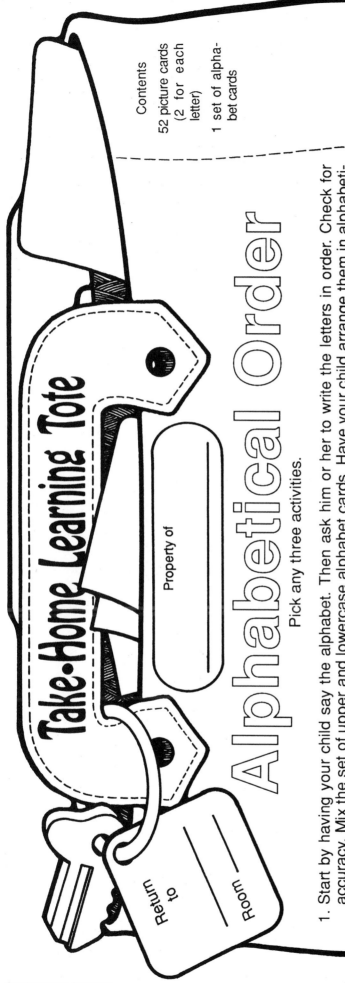

Take-Home Learning Tote

Property of
_____

Return to
_____
Room _____

Contents
52 picture cards (2 for each letter)
1 set of alpha-bet cards

Please be sure to return all contents. Thank you!

Alphabetical Order

Pick any three activities.

1. Start by having your child say the alphabet. Then ask him or her to write the letters in order. Check for accuracy. Mix the set of upper and lowercase alphabet cards. Have your child arrange them in alphabetical order.

2. Ask your child to sort the picture cards according to the beginning letter. Put the twenty-six sets of pictures in alphabetical order.

3. Write your family members' names on separate small pieces of paper. Have your child arrange them in alphabetical order. Add the names of aunts, uncles and cousins. Arrange this longer list in alphabetical order. If two or more names begin with the same letter, show how to alphabetize by also using the second letter.

4. Choose three words that start with the same letter (bat, box, be; jar, jet, jump; etc.) Write each one on a small piece of paper. Let your child alphabetize the words using the second and possibly the third letters as well as the first letter.

5. Using all fifty-two picture cards, turn them facedown. Have your child draw one card at a time and start placing the cards in alphabetical order. Show how to leave open space if pictures that are drawn are far apart in the alphabet such as:

b	f	m	w

6. Ask your child to write friends' names on separate pieces of paper. See if your child can put them in alphabetical order without any assistance.

GA1471

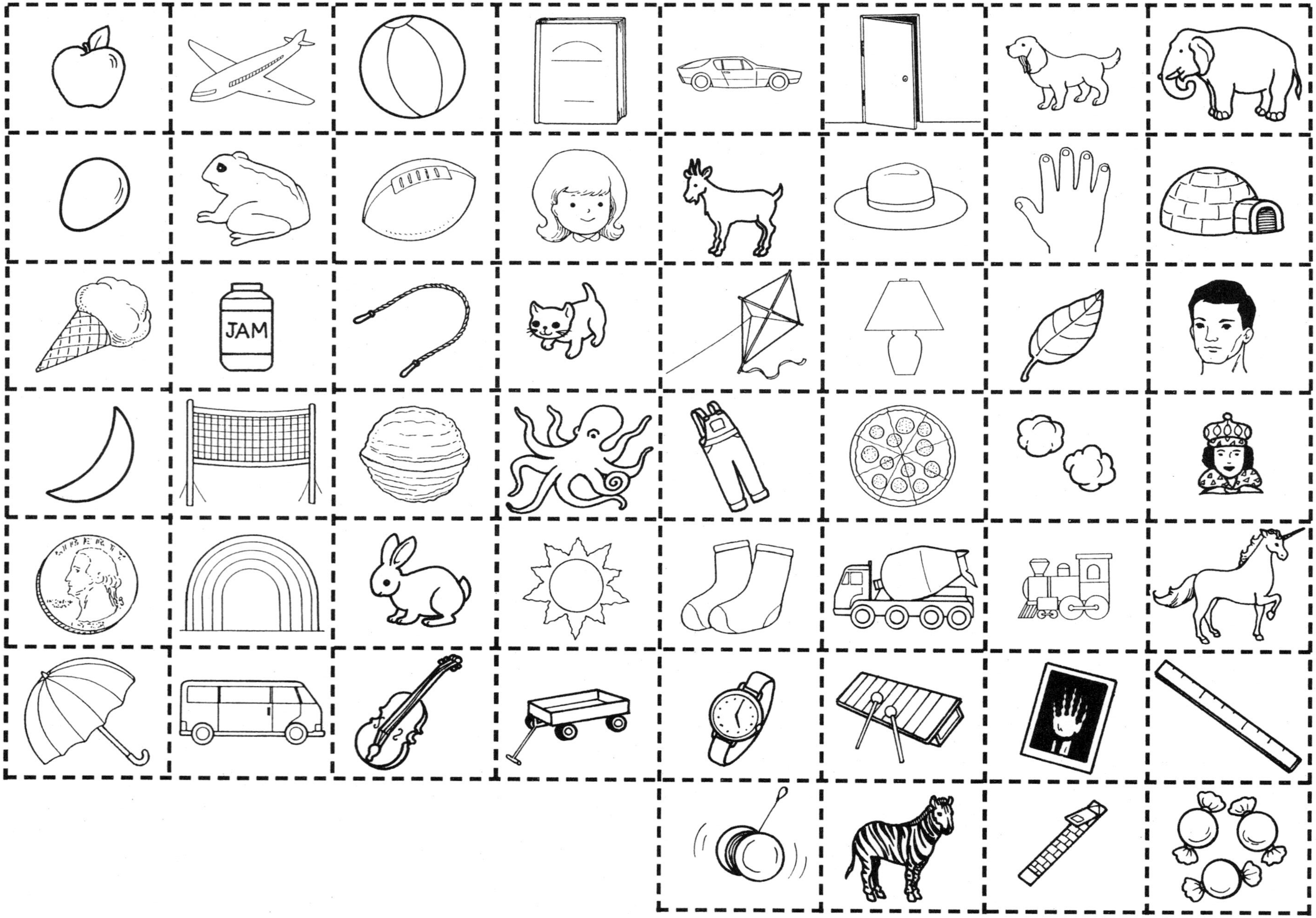

Directions: Reproduce this page. Color the illustrations if you wish. Laminate and cut cards apart to yield fifty-two cards.

50

GA1471

Aa Bb Cc Dd

Ee Ff Gg Hh

Ii Jj Kk Ll

Mm Nn Oo Pp

Qq Rr Ss Tt

Uu Vv Ww Xx

Yy Zz

Directions: Reproduce this page. Laminate and cut cards apart.

GA1471

Take-Home Learning Tote

Property of _____

Return to _____
Room _____

52

GA1471

Nouns and Verbs

Pick any three activities.

1. Talk about the difference between nouns and verbs. Explain that *nouns* are words that name things or people such as *table, chair, toy or John or Elizabeth*. *Verbs* are action words such as *run, jump, play or eat*. Ask your child to name several nouns and several verbs.

2. Have your child read the word cards. Sort them into groups of nouns and verbs.

3. Turn all noun cards facedown in one pile. Turn all verb cards facedown in a separate pile. Have your child draw one word from each pile. Ask him or her to create a sentence using both words.

4. Ask your child to say any sentence. Print it clearly so your child can read it easily. Identify which words in the sentences are nouns and which are verbs.

5. Using the fill-in-the-blank sentence page and the word cards, ask your child to make sentences. Try several variations for each sentence.

6. Separate the noun and verb cards and place them faceup so all cards can be read. Make up noun-verb phrases such as *boys run, friends dance, girls draw*, etc.

Contents

10 noun word cards

10 verb word cards

1 fill-in-the-sentence page

Please be sure to return all contents. Thank you!

run

boys

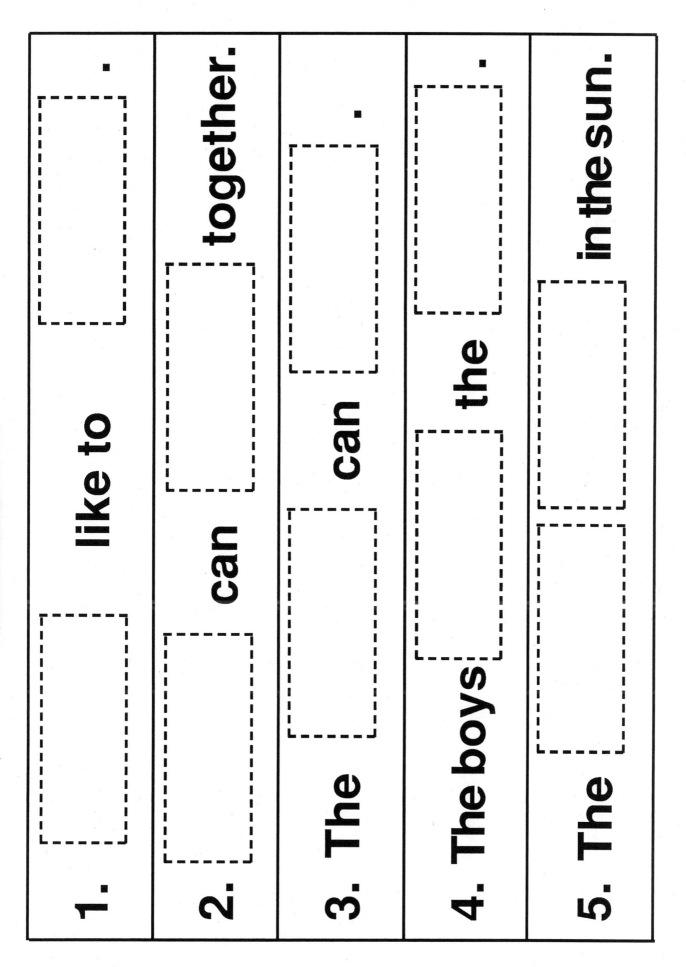

1. [ ] like to [ ] .

2. [ ] can together.

3. The [ ] can [ ] .

4. The boys [ ] the [ ] .

5. The [ ] in the sun.

Directions: Reproduce this page. Laminate and cut words apart to yield twenty cards.

GA1471

friends	cat	wash	climbs
birds	boys	sing	run
monkey	rabbit	watch	hops
mothers	girls	plays	dance
fathers	children	draw	walk

Directions: Reproduce this page. Laminate and cut words apart to yield twenty cards.

GA1471

Take-Home Learning Tote

Property of
_____

Return to
_____

Room
_____

Contractions

Pick any three activities.

1. Use the contraction flash cards. Ask your child to read the flash cards to you. Tell your child that the apostrophe represents missing letters. Ask your child to figure out the two words represented by the contraction and the missing letters that would be in the place of the apostrophe. Help your child become familiar with the terms *apostrophe* and *contraction*.

2. Ask your child to match the contraction cards with the word cards that the contractions represent.

3. Place all contraction cards facedown in one pile, two-word cards in another. Select a card from each pile. If they are a contraction-match, keep the pair of cards and take another turn. If they are not a match, replace each card facedown in the pile. (Insert at random in the pile; do not place both cards at the bottoms of each pile as they will again appear as a non-match.) Players take turns trying to pick a match. Continue until all matches are made. The player with the most matching pairs wins.

4. Make up a sentence using one of the two-word cards. Ask your child to find the word card you used and to find the contraction for it. Ask your child to restate your sentence using the contraction.

5. Ask your child to write any sentence using a contraction. Ask your child to identify the contraction and say the words the contractions represent.

6. Place all cards facedown. You pick a card. Make up a sentence using the word(s) on the card. Ask your child to restate your sentence using the opposite form that you used in your sentence. For example: You have chosen the card *don't*. You say to your child, "Boys *don't* wear dresses." Your child should restate your sentence: "Boys *do not* wear dresses." If you chose the card *could not*, your sentence might be: "Johnny *could not* climb the big tree." Your child should say, "Johnny *couldn't* climb the big tree."

Contents

15 contraction cards

15 two-word cards

Please be sure to return all contents. Thank you!

55

GA1471

aren't	won't	don't
isn't	haven't	can't
wasn't	hasn't	let's
weren't	shouldn't	wouldn't
it's	doesn't	couldn't

Contractions

Directions: Reproduce this page and the following page. Laminate and cut cards apart to yield fifteen on each page.

GA1471

are not	is not	was not	were not
			it is
will not	have not	has not	should not
			does not
do not	can not	let us	would not
			could not

GA1471

Take-Home Learning Tote

Property of
_____

Return to
_____
Room _____

Contents

24 word cards

24 pictures to make 12 compound puzzle pairs

Please be sure to return all contents. Thank you!

Compound Words

Pick any three activities.

1. Talk about the meaning of *compound words* with your child. Explain that it is a combination of two words that join to become one larger word. The larger word has its own meaning. Give examples such as *rain + drop* make *raindrop, hot + dog* make *hotdog*, and *bath + room* make *bathroom*.

2. Spread out the word cards, faceup, in random order. Ask your child to select two words that will make a compound word. Use the compound word in a sentence. Repeat until all sets of words are made into compound words.

3. Mix the twenty-four puzzle pieces. Ask your child to match the pairs of puzzle pieces; then match the compound word card to each pair.

4. Put all the word cards in a bag. Ask your child to draw out two cards. If these two cards make a compound word, do not replace in the bag. If they do not make a compound word, put the cards back in the bag. Shake the bag to mix the cards. Pick another two cards. Continue until your child has used all the cards to make compound words.

5. Give your child one or two magazines to be cut up. Ask him or her to find pictures that are examples of compound words and cut them out. Help your child to find one picture (foot) on one page and another picture of a word (ball) on another page to make the word *football*. This is a creative and challenging activity; give suggestions and guide your child as you work together.

GA1471

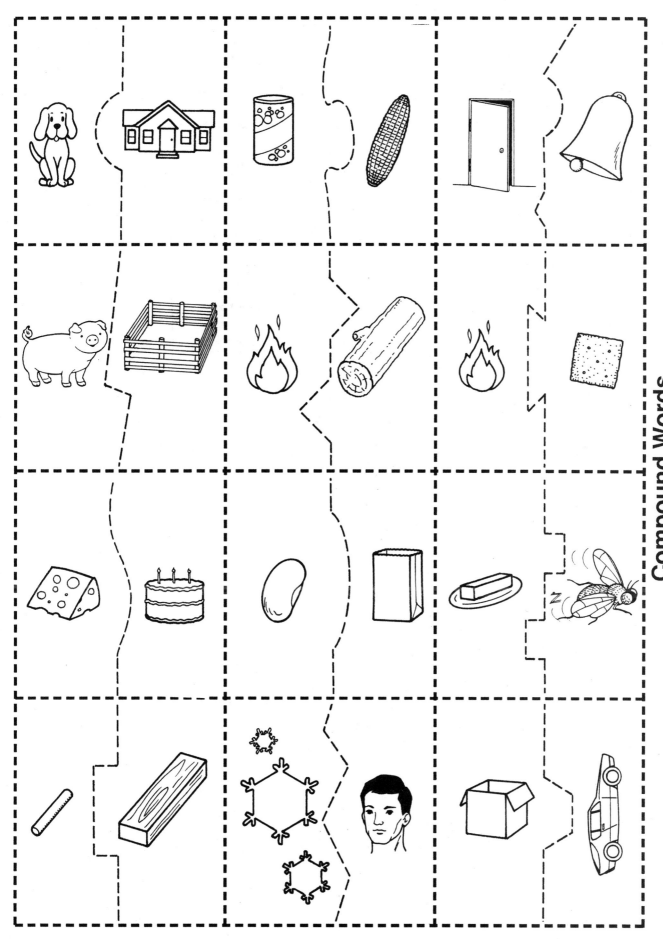

Compound Words

Directions: Reproduce this page. Color the illustrations. Laminate and cut apart into twelve cards; then cut each card to make a puzzle pair.

59

cracker	fire	house	dog
cake	cheese	corn	pop
bag	bean	car	box
fly	butter	bell	door
board	chalk	pen	pig
man	snow	wood	fire

60

Directions: Reproduce this page. Laminate and cut words apart to yield twenty-four cards.

GA1471

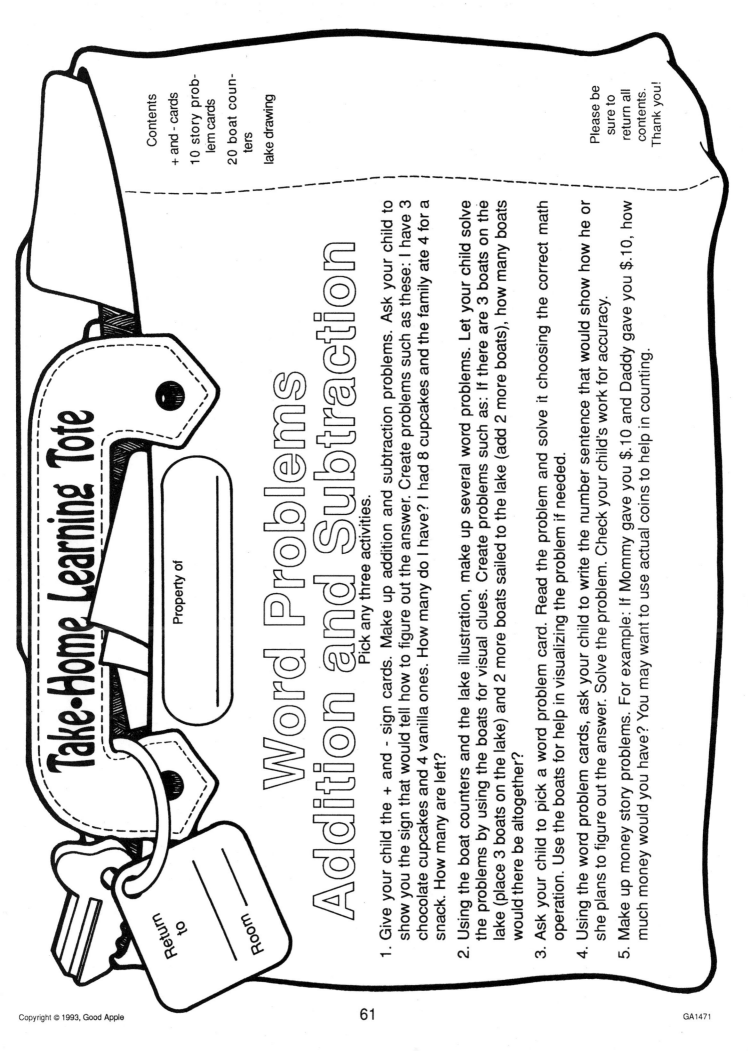

Take-Home Learning Tote

Property of _____

Return to _____

Room _____

Word Problems
Addition and Subtraction

Pick any three activities.

1. Give your child the + and - sign cards. Make up addition and subtraction problems. Ask your child to show you the sign that would tell how to figure out the answer. Create problems such as these: I have 3 chocolate cupcakes and 4 vanilla ones. How many do I have? I had 8 cupcakes and the family ate 4 for a snack. How many are left?

2. Using the boat counters and the lake illustration, make up several word problems. Let your child solve the problems by using the boats for visual clues. Create problems such as: If there are 3 boats on the lake (place 3 boats on the lake) and 2 more boats sailed to the lake (add 2 more boats), how many boats would there be altogether?

3. Ask your child to pick a word problem card. Read the problem and solve it choosing the correct math operation. Use the boats for help in visualizing the problem if needed.

4. Using the word problem cards, ask your child to write the number sentence that would show how he or she plans to figure out the answer. Solve the problem. Check your child's work for accuracy.

5. Make up money story problems. For example: If Mommy gave you $.10 and Daddy gave you $.10, how much money would you have? You may want to use actual coins to help in counting.

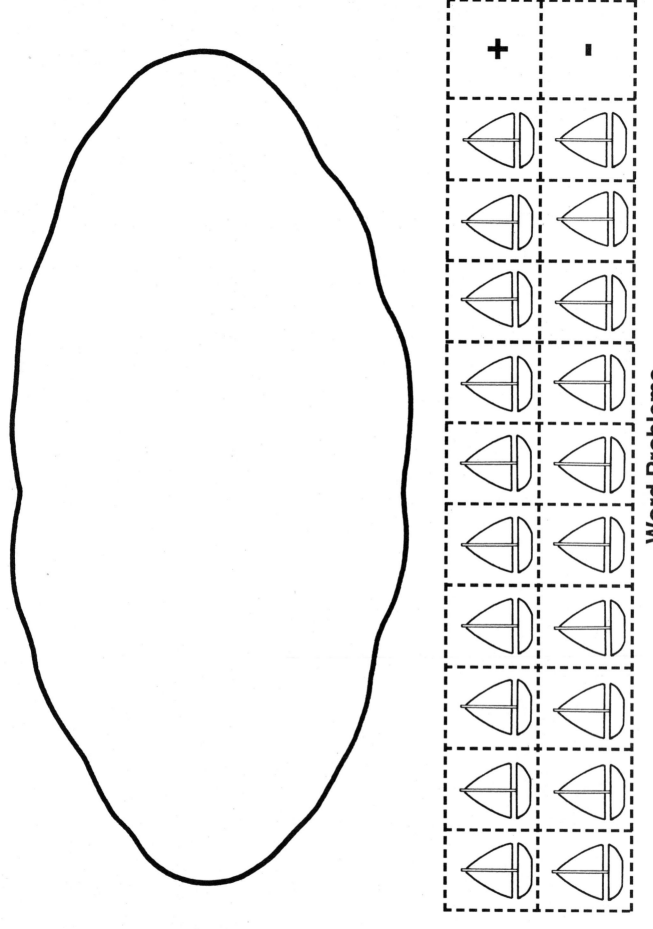

Word Problems

Directions: Reproduce this page. Cut on dotted line. Color and laminate lake illustration. Laminate strip of boat counters and + and - signs. Cut apart after laminating.

62

GA1471

Early in the morning, there were 5 boats on the lake. Later in the morning 7 more boats came to sail. How many boats were on the lake then?

6 families put their boats on the lake. Then it started to rain. 3 families decided to leave and go home. How many boats were left on the lake?

8 boats were sailing on the lake. 7 more boats joined them in a race. How many boats were in the race?

15 boats had been sailing all day. At 4 o'clock, 9 sailboats left. How many boats continued to sail?

Amy had 6 toy boats. Evan had 7 toy boats. They sailed all their boats together at the park lake. How many boats did they sail?

Michelle had 20 little toy boats to share with her friend. She gave Jeff 10 boats to play with. How many did she have left to play with?

In the morning there were 4 sailboats on the lake. In the afternoon, 10 more boats sailed in. How many boats were on the lake?

There were 16 boats on East Lake. 7 families decided to take their boats to West Lake. How many boats were left on East Lake?

There were 5 sailboats with white sails and 9 sailboats with colored sails. How many sailboats were there all together?

There were 8 boats on the lake. Half the boats left. How many remained?

63

GA1471

Take-Home Learning Tote

Property of _____

Return to _____

Room _____

Contents

6 sets of family fact math cards; 4 per set for a total of 24 cards

10 monkey and 10 elephant circus train cards

Please be sure to return all contents. Thank you!

Turnaround Family Math Facts

Pick any three activities.

1. Discuss what a turnaround math fact is. Show the number sentence: 4 + 3 = 7. Explain that there are three other ways to use the *same* numbers to make *different* number sentences. Show the other facts to go with 4 + 3 = 7 (3 + 4 = 7, 7 - 3 = 4 and 7 - 4 = 3). Write another turnaround fact. Ask your child to write the other three number sentences.

2. Select an *addition* number sentence card from the set of twenty-four cards. Ask your child to find the other three turnaround facts that go with the addition card. Work to solve all four problems. Use counters if needed. Repeat using another addition card.

3. Using the monkey and elephant cards, make an animal train. You may select two monkey cards and three elephant cards. Ask your child to write the number sentence that tells how many animals are on the train . . . 2 + 3 = 5. Then ask your child to write the other three number sentences in the turnaround family. Make up different problems for your child to solve.

4. Select a *subtraction* number sentence card from the set of twenty-four cards. Make up a word problem using the card you selected. (9 - 3 = . . . There were 9 elephants on the train. 3 left to be in a circus parade. How many elephants were left on the train?) Without letting your child see the card you selected, have him or her write the number sentence for the story problem you made up. Compare the card to what your child has written for accuracy. Write the other three turnaround facts.

5. Ask your child to find all the "matches" in the turnaround math fact cards to create six sets. Use the monkey and elephant cards to show the solutions for extra practice.

GA1471

$2 + 3 =$	$3 + 2 =$	$5 - 2 =$	$5 - 3 =$		
$4 + 1 =$	$1 + 4 =$	$5 - 1 =$	$5 - 4 =$		
$6 + 3 =$	$3 + 6 =$	$9 - 6 =$	$9 - 3 =$		
$5 + 4 =$	$4 + 5 =$	$9 - 4 =$	$9 - 5 =$		
$7 + 3 =$	$3 + 7 =$	$10 - 7 =$	$10 - 3 =$		
$3 + 4 =$	$4 + 3 =$	$7 - 3 =$	$7 - 4 =$		

Turnaround Family Math Facts

Directions: Reproduce this page. Laminate and cut apart to yield twenty-four cards.

GA1471

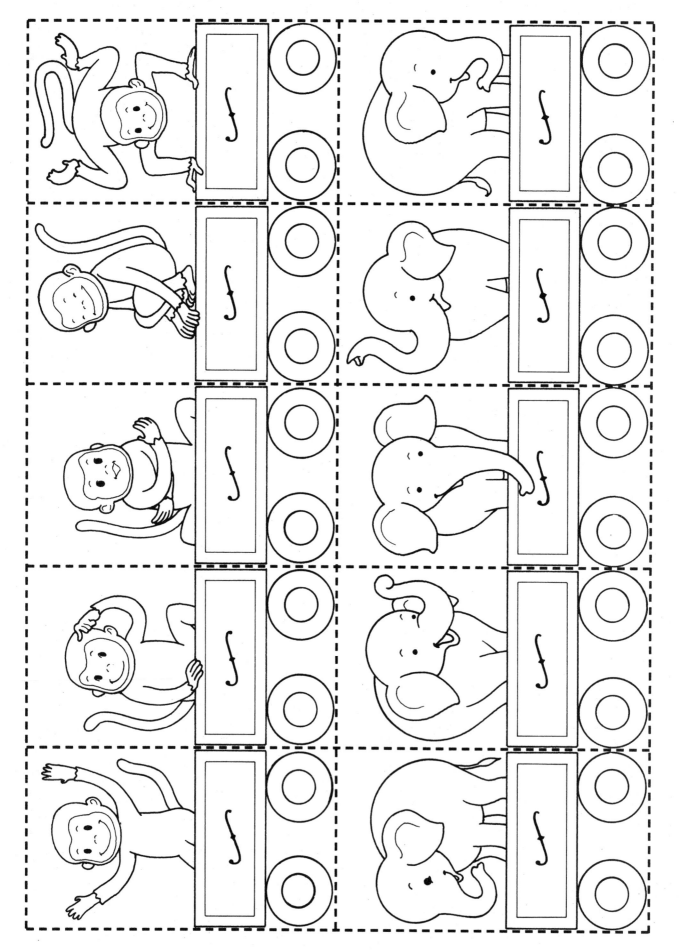

Directions: Reproduce this page *twice* to yield ten monkey and ten elephant circus train cards. Color the cards. Laminate and cut apart.

66

GA1471

Take-Home Learning Tote

Property of _____

Return to _____

Room _____

Place Value

Pick any three activities.

1. Ask your child to group the counters (toothpicks or straws) into sets of ten. Put a rubber band around each set of ten. Count by tens.

2. Give your child any number of counters between 11-29. Ask your child to group into tens and ones. Put rubber bands around each group of ten. Count and tell how many counters there are. Ask your child to write the number. Now compare the number of sets of ten to the numeral in the tens place; compare the number of counters without a rubber band to the numeral in the ones place. Use the terms *tens and ones place* with your child. Ask him or her to identify which is the tens place, which is the ones place.

24 = ||||||||| |||||||||| ||||

3. Give your child any number of toothpicks. Ask your child to group them into hundreds, tens, and ones. Write the number that shows how many counters. Also, show your child how to group ten tens into one group of one hundred if you give more than one hundred counters. Put one rubber band around ten sets of ten. This will be a good visual aid.

4. Group the counters into ten sets of ten. Write any number between 1-150. Ask your child to represent that number using the sets of tens and single counters.

5. Using a dollar, dimes, and pennies, ask your child to represent different numbers. Talk about the pennies representing the ones place, dimes the tens place, and the dollar the hundreds place. DO NOT USE TWO NICKELS IN PLACE OF A DIME.

Take-Home Learning Tote

Property of

_____

Return to _____

Room _____

Contents

number cards
0-20

Please be
sure to
return all
contents.
Thank you!

Before, Between and After
Missing Numbers

Pick any three activities.

1. Using any three consecutive number cards, place them in order for your child to see. Remove the middle number and mix it with the remaining number cards. Ask your child to find the missing number and replace it in the correct spot. After this demonstration put up two number cards that have a missing number between them. Leave a space for the missing card. Ask your child what number goes between the two number cards shown. Place the correct number card in the open space.

2. Place the number cards in sequential order 0-20. Remove all the odd-numbered cards. Mix in random order and place faceup. Ask your child to replace the numbers in the correct spaces. Ask your child to replace specific numbers. For example: Find the number card that goes between 16 and 18, and place it in the correct space. Continue until all numbers are in correct sequential order. Play again, removing the even-numbered cards. Play again, removing any ten number cards.

3. Put all number cards in a bag. Ask your child to draw out one card. Your child tells you the number and the number that comes immediately before and after that number. If correct, let your child keep the number card. If incorrect, put the number back in the bag to try again. Continue until all numbers are out of the bag.

4. Turn all number cards facedown in a random row. Ask your child to pick one card. *This is your starting point.* Turn all cards faceup. Starting with the first card drawn, your child must put the cards in sequential order by putting cards to the left and to the right of the card that was drawn until all cards are in the sequence 0-20.

5. Make up before, between and after statements. Let your child figure out the number you are thinking about by listening to your clues. For example: I am thinking of a number that comes before 7 and after 5. What is the number? I am thinking of a number between 11 and 13. What is the number?

68

GA1471

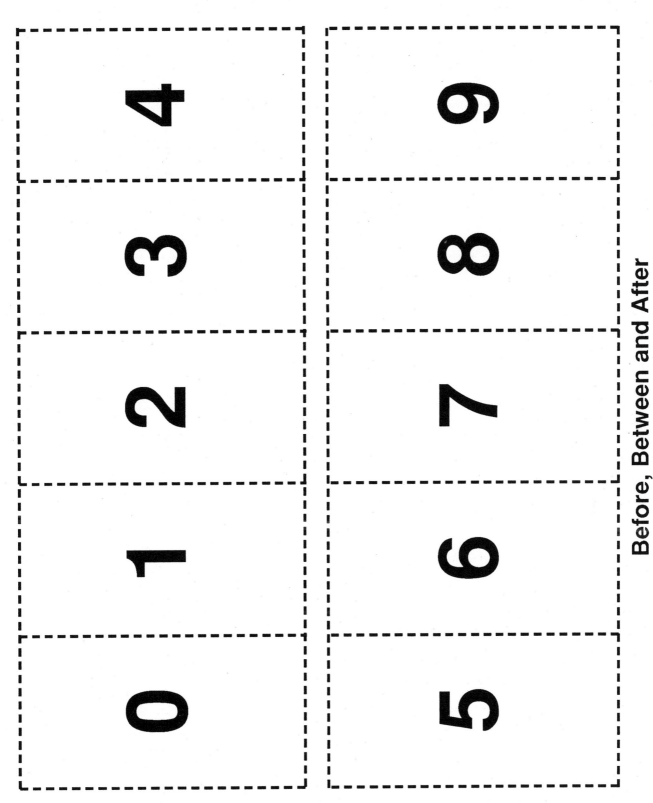

Before, Between and After

Directions: Reproduce this page and the following page. Laminate and cut cards apart.

15 14 13 12 11 10

20 19 18 17 16

70

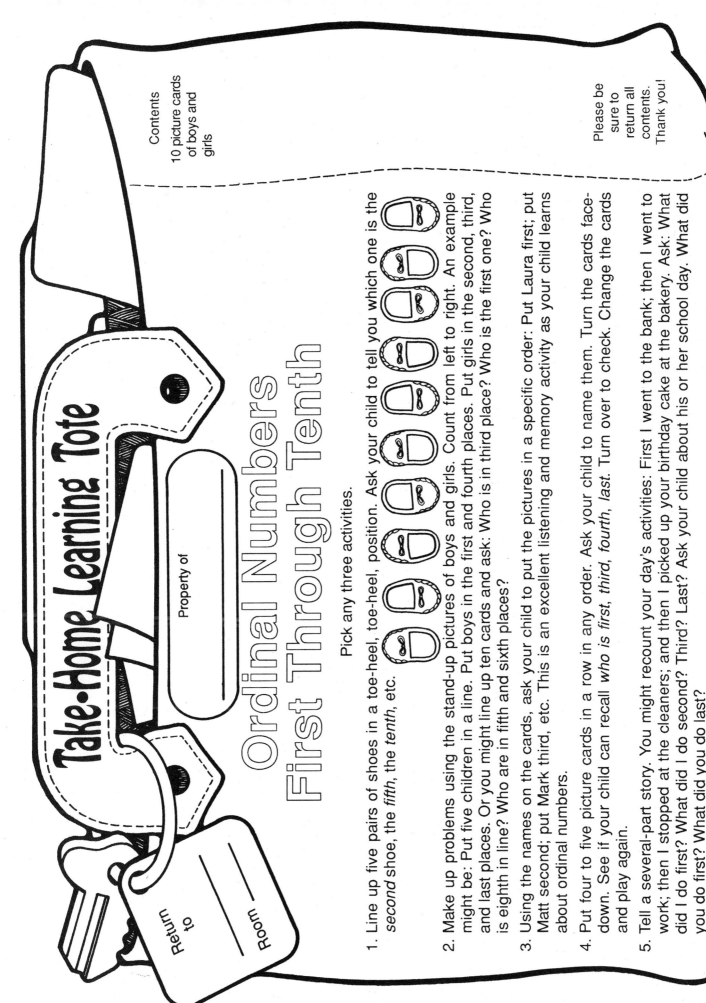

Take-Home Learning Tote

Property of _____

Return to _____

Room _____

Ordinal Numbers
First Through Tenth

Pick any three activities.

1. Line up five pairs of shoes in a toe-heel, toe-heel, position. Ask your child to tell you which one is the *second* shoe, the *fifth*, the *tenth*, etc.

2. Make up problems using the stand-up pictures of boys and girls. Count from left to right. An example might be: Put five children in a line. Put boys in the first and fourth places. Put girls in the second, third, and last places. Or you might line up ten cards and ask: Who is in third place? Who is eighth in line? Who are in fifth and sixth places?

3. Using the names on the cards, ask your child to put the pictures in a specific order: Put Laura first; put Matt second; put Mark third, etc. This is an excellent listening and memory activity as your child learns about ordinal numbers.

4. Put four to five picture cards in a row in any order. Ask your child to name them. Turn the cards face-down. Ask your child can recall *who is first, third, fourth, last.* Turn over to check. Change the cards and play again.

5. Tell a several-part story. You might recount your day's activities: First I went to the bank; then I went to work; then I stopped at the cleaners; and then I picked up your birthday cake at the bakery. Ask: What did I do first? What did I do second? Third? Last? Ask your child about his or her school day. What did you do first? What did you do last?

GA1471

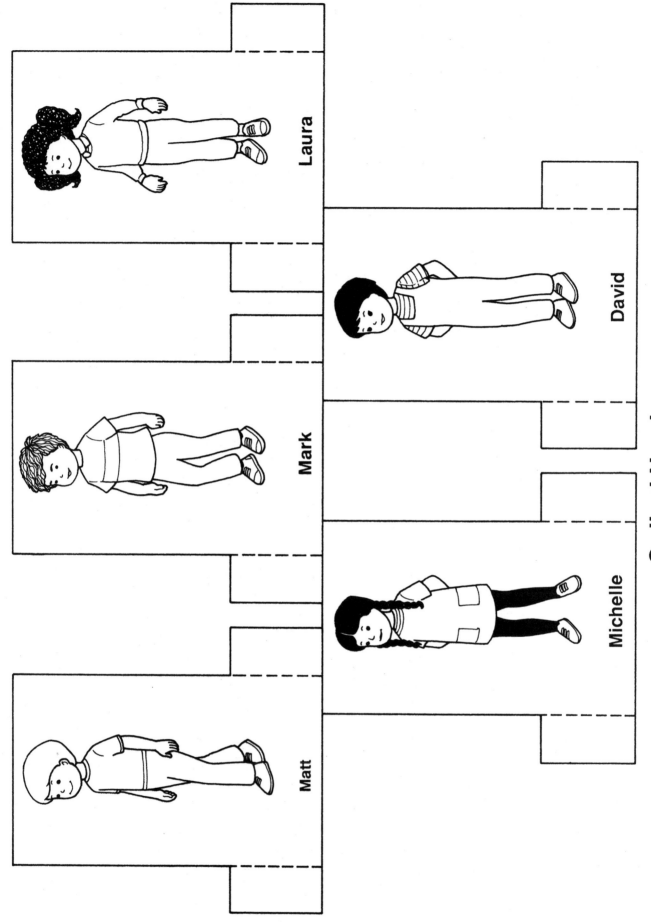

Laura

David

Mark

Michelle

Matt

Ordinal Numbers

Directions: Reproduce this page and the following page. Color the illustrations if you wish, laminate and cut out each card. Fold back on dotted lines to create stand-ups.

GA1471

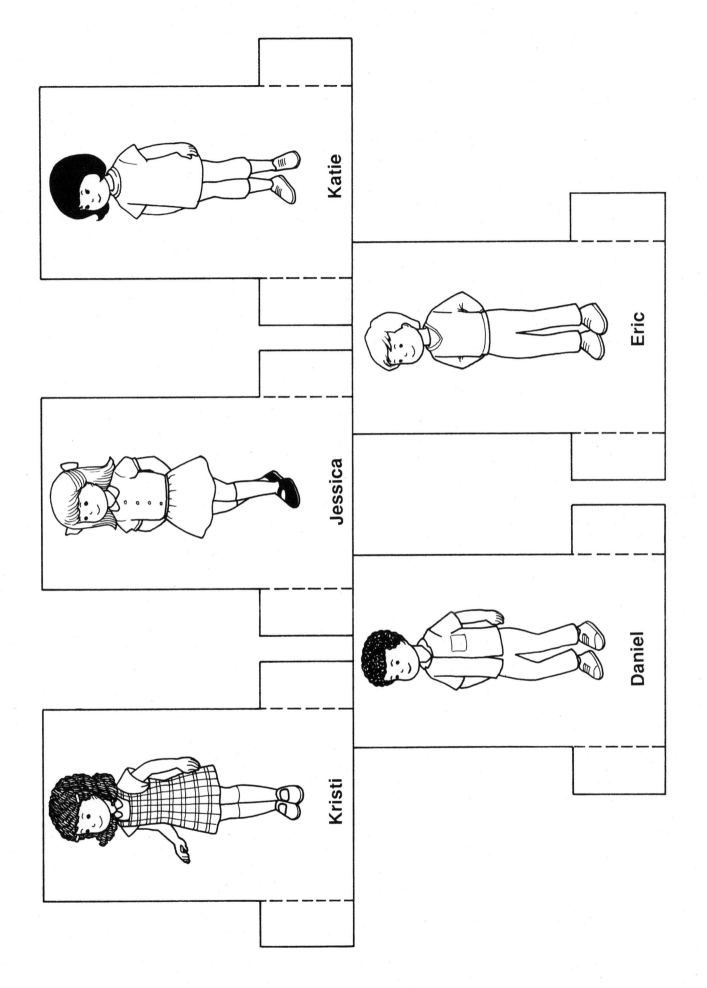

Katie

Eric

Jessica

Daniel

Kristi

73

Take-Home Learning Tote

Property of _____

Return to _____

Room _____

Fractions—1/2, 1/3, 1/4

Pick any three activities.

1. Discuss with your child how fractions are *equal* parts of a whole. Use the circles and fractional pieces as a visual aid. Discuss the fact that just because something is cut into four pieces that does not necessarily mean it is cut into fourths.

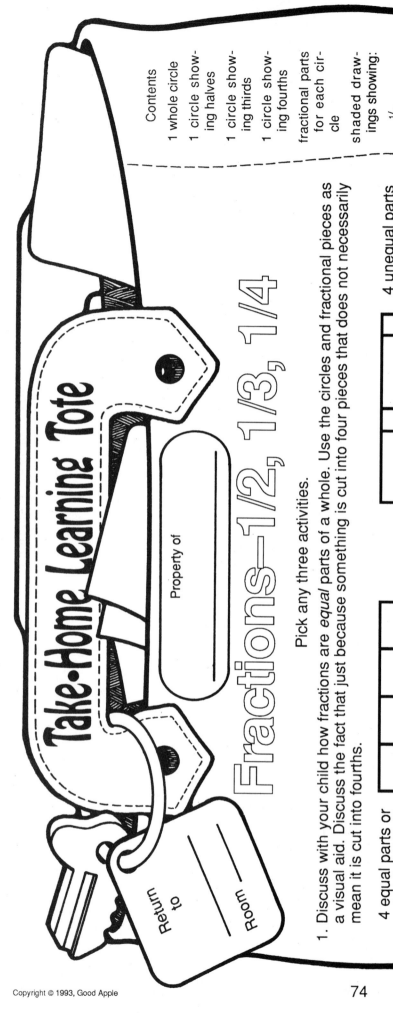

4 equal parts or *fourths*

4 unequal parts

2. Using the fractional pieces of the circles, ask your child to identify the pieces using the terms *half, third,* and *fourth*. Show your child how to write a fraction.

3. Give your child two halves, three thirds, and four fourths and ask him or her to make a whole circle with each set of fractional pieces. Take away ¹/₄. How many are left? Write the fraction. Take away ¹/₃. How many are left? Write the fraction.

4. Using the shaded pictures of the circles, ask your child to tell you what fractional part of each circle is shaded. Ask what part is not shaded. Write the fraction.

5. Use twelve pennies. Ask your child to separate them into halves. Point out that there are two equal groups of six. Separate into thirds and show three equal groups. Do the same for fourths.

6. Give your child twelve pennies. Ask your child to give you ¹/₂ of the pennies, ¹/₃ of the pennies, ¹/₄ of the pennies, ²/₃ of the pennies and ³/₄ of the pennies. If your child has any difficulty with this, separate into halves, thirds, and fourths again. Show how two groups of the pennies when separated into thirds equals ²/₃, etc. This would be a good time to show that ¹/₂ = ²/₄.

Contents

1 whole circle

1 circle showing halves

1 circle showing thirds

1 circle showing fourths

fractional parts for each circle

shaded drawings showing:

¹/₂

¹/₃

²/₃

¹/₄

²/₄

³/₄

Please be sure to return all contents. Thank you!

74

GA1471

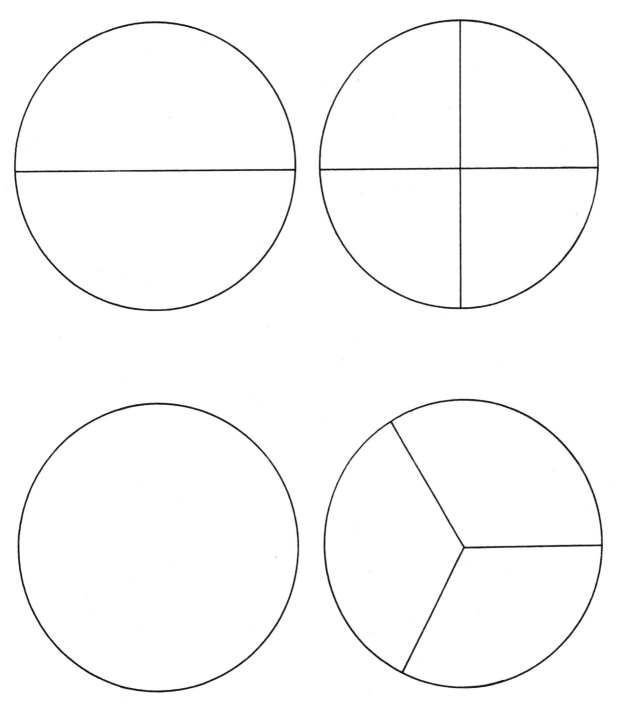

Fractions

Directions: Reproduce this page and the following page. Cut out whole circles on this page. Cut out fractional pieces of circles and six shaded circles on the next page. You may want to color in the shaded parts for emphasis. Laminate all pieces.

GA1471

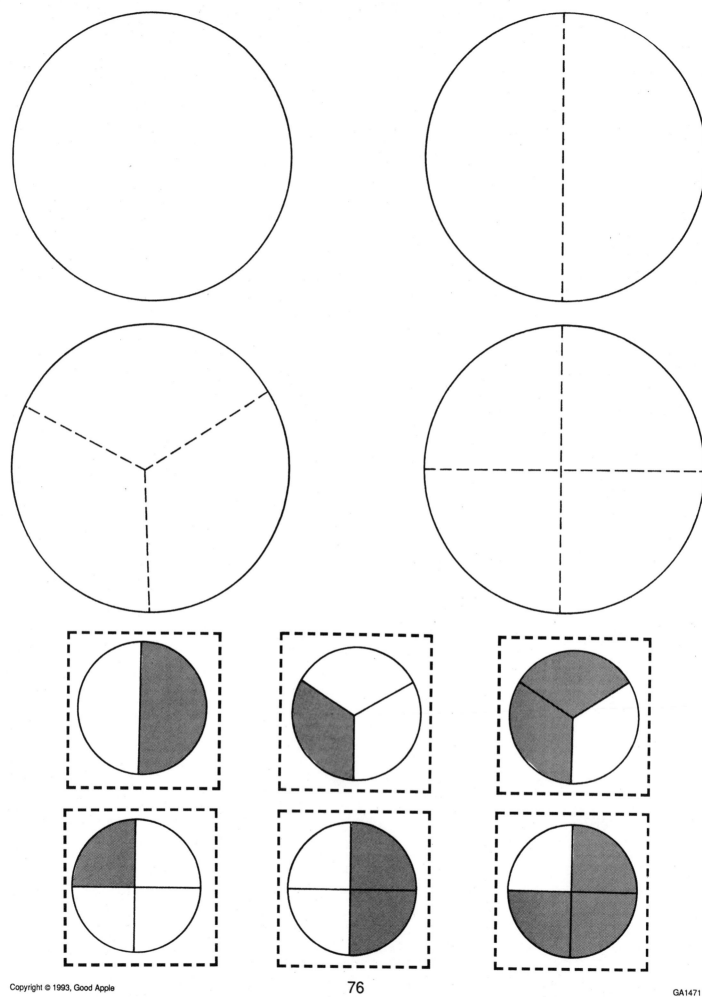

76

GA1471

Contents

1 10-inch ruler

1 20-cm ruler

1 24-inch piece of yarn

6 snake drawings

Please be sure to return all contents. Thank you!

Take-Home Learning Tote

Property of _____

Return to _____

Room _____

Measurement

Pick any three activities.

1. Ask your child to use the 10-inch ruler to measure different items in your house. Select items such as a book, a large envelope, a photograph, a small box, a windowsill, a doorway, etc. Record each finding. Then measure the same items using the 20-centimeter ruler.

2. Discuss with your child the following standards used in measuring:

   12 inches = 1 foot   3 feet = 1 yard

   10 centimeters = 1 decimeter   10 decimeters = 1 meter

   Using a 12-inch ruler and a yardstick, show that 3 feet = 1 yard.

3. Ask your child to measure the couch, the table, the television, and the refrigerator using the 24-inch piece of yarn enclosed. Show your child how to hold the yarn at the end and move the beginning of it to continue measuring a long object. This is measuring in *nonstandard units*. For fun, let your child use his or her shoe as a unit of measurement. Measure several items in the house. How many shoes wide is the bathroom? The front doorway? The kitchen? Record your results.

4. Use the six snake pictures and the yarn to measure curved lines. Ask your child to estimate how long each wiggly snake is. Lay the yarn on the snake following the curves. Be sure the end of the yarn starts at the mouth of the snake. Hold the place on the yarn where the snake ends. Measure that section of the yarn. Compare the estimate with the actual measurement. See how estimates improve with repeated practice.

GA1471

Measurement

Directions: Reproduce this page and the following page. Color each snake. Laminate and cut out the six strips of snakes.

78

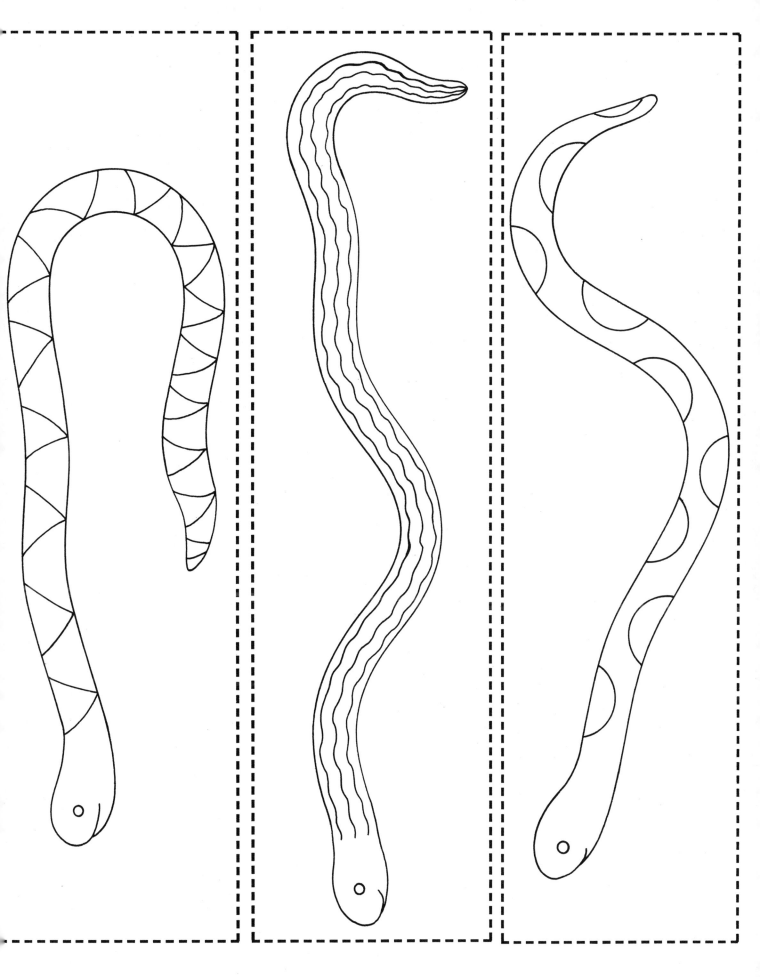

Centimeters

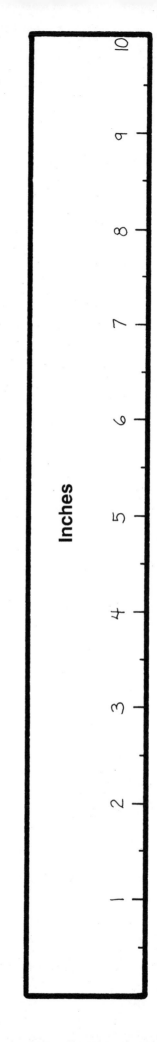

Inches

Directions: Reproduce this page. Use manila tagboard to give more strength, as these rulers will be handled frequently. Cut out each ruler. Laminate in addition to reproducing on tagboard. (You may want to make two to three extra sets of rulers to replace any that become used and worn.)

80

GA1471

Take-Home Learning Tote

Property of
_____

Return
to
_____
_____ Room

81

GA1471

Contents

6 picture cards:
candy bar
football
doll
coat
bicycle
television

6 price tags:
$.50
$10.00
$12.00
$39.00
$75.00
$300.00

12 money cards

Please be
sure to
return all
contents.
Thank you!

Money

Pick any three activities.

Adults: You will need ten pennies, five nickels, two dimes, four quarters and a one-dollar bill to do these activities.

1. Mix the coins together. Ask your child to sort the coins into groups and tell you the value of each coin and each group of coins. Discuss how different coins have the same value. Show ten pennies. Then ask "What other coins would be the same as ten pennies?" If your child shows two nickels, ask if there is a third way to equal ten cents. Work with your child to show one nickel and five pennies as another way. Make up other coin-value problems.

2. Ask your child to use the *fewest* coins possible to show the following amounts: $.07, $.25, $.58, $1.10. Make up other amounts to show.

3. Ask your child to match the pictures with the correct price tag cards. Estimate which cards might tell the approximate price of the item. Are there any two items that might cost about the same? (football, doll) What item is the least expensive? What item is the most expensive?

4. Use the twelve money cards and all the coins listed above. Place the coins aside and use this as "the bank." Place the cards facedown. Ask your child to select one card and take coins from the bank to show the amount on the card. If correct, the coins are returned to the bank and another card is selected. If incorrect, work with your child to correct the error. Leave the card for another try. Repeat until all cards have been used.

$.50

$10.00

$12.00

$39.00

$75.00

$300.00

Chocolate Bar

Money

Directions: Reproduce this page. Color the illustrations. Laminate and cut cards apart.

GA1471

$.25	24¢
$.06	8¢
$.15	17¢
$.21	4¢
$.03	10¢
$.12	19¢

GA1471

Directions: Reproduce this page. Laminate and cut cards apart.

Take-Home Learning Tote

Property of _____

Return
to _____

_____ Room

Contents

3 graphs

Please be
sure to
return all
contents.
Thank you!

Graphing and Tallying

Pick any three activities.

Adults: Please use crayon for marking on graphs. Please wipe clean before returning to tote bag. Thank you.

1. You will need a penny, pencil and paper. Draw two horizontal lines across the top of the paper. Designate one line for *heads* and one line for *tails*. Flip a penny twenty-five times. Make a tally mark (卅) on the appropriate line after each flip. Count the number of tally marks for heads and for tails. Transfer this information to the "Heads and Tails" graph by coloring in a square for each flip. Read the graph. Ask questions such as Which came up more—heads or tails? How many more times did heads come up than tails (or vice versa)?

2. Use a jump rope or a bouncing ball for this activity. Ask your child how many times he or she can jump or bounce without missing. Graph the first, second, third, fourth and fifth tries. Which one was your best? Your worst? Do this as a team with your child. One person colors a square as the other does the activity.

3. Write each family member's name on a sheet of paper. Ask your child to graph how many times the same letter appears in each name. Show your child how to strike through the letters of the name so you know the letter has been counted and colored on the graph. Add all letters of names for your family to the graph. How many *e*'s were there? How many *z*'s? How many *h*'s? Etc. What letter(s) appears most often? What letters do not appear at all?

Christina   William

GA1471

Heads and Tails

#1 Graph

	Heads	Tails

Jumps and Bounces

#2 Graph

1st Try					
2nd Try					
3rd Try					
4th Try					
5th Try					

Graphing and Tallying

Directions: Reproduce this page and the following page. Laminate. You may wish to check these graphs and replace them as needed if crayon marks build up and the graphs are difficult to see clearly.

GA1471

Letter Chart

A													
B													
C													
D													
E													
F													
G													
H													
I													
J													
K													
L													
M													
N													
O													
P													
Q													
R													
S													
T													
U													
V													
W													
X													
Y													
Z													

GA1471

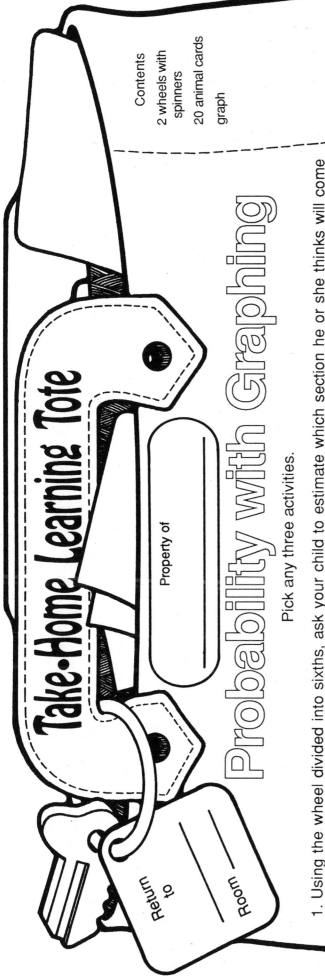

Contents
2 wheels with spinners
20 animal cards
graph

Please be sure to return all contents. Thank you!

Take-Home Learning Tote

Return to _____

Room _____

Probability With Graphing

Pick any three activities.

1. Using the wheel divided into sixths, ask your child to estimate which section he or she thinks will come up most often after spinning twenty times. Then spin the wheel twenty times and record the results of each spin by marking the appropriate animal box on the graph. After twenty spins check the graph to see which section came up most often. Was your guess correct?

2. Using the wheel divided into six unequal parts, ask your child to estimate which section he or she thinks will come up most often after twenty spins. Why? Discuss the fact that some sections are larger than others. How does this affect the estimate? Spin and record the results of each spin on the graph. Which section came up most often? Least often?

3. Discuss with your child that *probability* means "what probably will happen." It does not necessarily have to happen! If you flip a penny in the air ten times, it probably would land on heads half the time and tails half the time. Try the experiment by flipping several sets of ten. How many times did it take to get a 5:5 ratio of heads to tails? Let your child do the flipping and recording.

4. Use the twenty animal cards. Ask your child to put them in a small bag and shake it. Ask how many cards he or she thinks will land faceup and how many will land facedown when the bag is turned over and emptied. Record the guess. Empty the bag and check. How close was the estimate?

5. Use one monkey, two bird, three cat and five dog cards. Put the cards in a bag. Tell your child to draw out one card at a time, record what card was drawn, and put it back in the bag. Make twenty draws. What card was drawn most often? Least often? Why? Change the number of dogs, cats, birds and monkeys. Before drawing, ask your child to estimate which card will be drawn out most often. Draw twenty times. Record and check your results.

GA1471

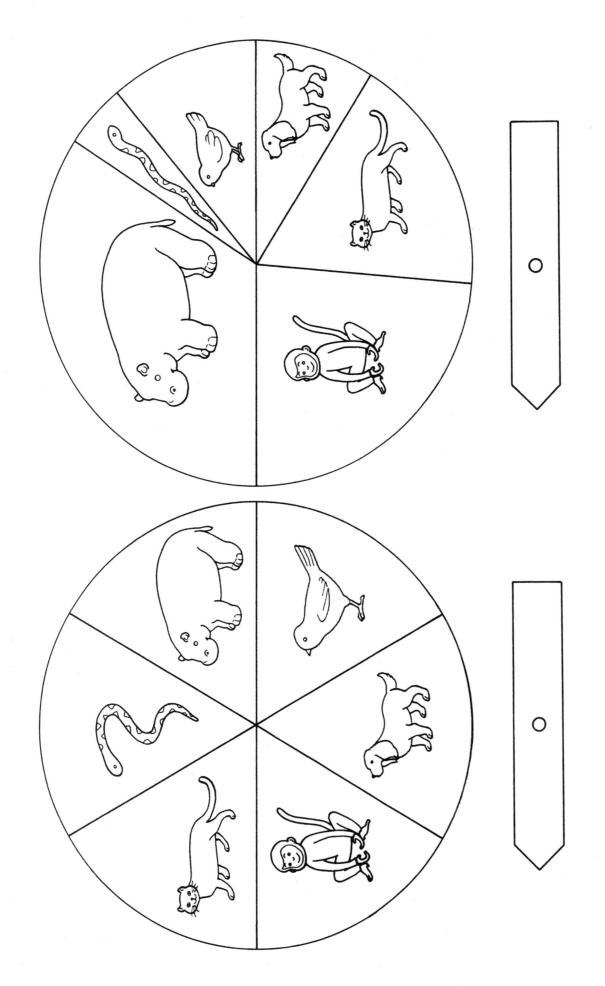

Probability with Graphing

Directions: Reproduce this page. Color each animal section the same color on both circles. Cut out circles and spinners. Laminate circles and spinners. Attach a spinner to the center of each circle with a fastener/brad and check to see that the spinner moves freely.

GA1471

Directions: Reproduce this page. Laminate cards and cut apart to yield twenty cards.

89

GA1471

90

Directions: Reproduce this page. Color the sections with animal illustrations on the left to match the colored sections on the two wheels. This will help children to mark the appropriate box. Laminate. You may wish to check this graph and replace it as needed if crayon marks build up and the graph is difficult to see clearly.